The Young Country Doctor Book 9
Bilbury Relish

Vernon Coleman

Dedication: To Antoinette

You make my world go round and the freehold to my heart is yours for eternity.

Dear Reader

I have been asked to remind you that the Bilbury books are all set in the 1970s and although this book is being written well into the 21st century, I am writing about things that happened nearly half a century ago. Please remember that medical knowledge and customs were very different then.

Some older readers will remember those distant days with fondness but many younger readers will probably find it difficult to imagine living in a world without mobile telephones, computers and the mass of gadgets and conveniences which we all now take for granted.

Finally, I should also point out that I take the principle of confidentiality very seriously and so none of the people or situations described in this book are recognisable.

Welcome back to Bilbury.

Vernon Coleman
Bilbury Grange
Bilbury
Devon
England

The Children's Party

Bilbury is a wonderful place for children. The lanes are safe because there is relatively little traffic and children can be allowed to cycle for miles around the countryside. There are moors to roam, woods to explore and rivers in which to swim or plan pirate adventures. The coast, complete with rocky coves and fine beaches, is just a short cycle ride away and the only strangers to be seen are usually breathless hikers carrying rucksacks and worn out by the incessant ups and downs of the North Devon countryside.

For children, the lifestyle is as healthy as you can imagine. There are the occasional grazed knees and bee stings to be dealt with, and once every couple of years an over-adventurous child will fall off a bicycle or out of a tree and breaks a bone. But, on the whole, it would be difficult to find a safer place for a growing child.

Just occasionally, however, nature has a habit of reminding us all that life in the countryside can have its own special dangers.

I was cutting the grass in the orchard one beautiful, sunny Sunday afternoon when Patsy, who had been weeding the flowerbeds near to the house, came running down the garden to tell me that Mrs Ermentrude Pinchbeck had telephoned, in a panic, to ask me to go round to her house straight away. There were, she had told Patsy, twelve or fifteen children suffering from terrible burns on their hands and faces. Patsy told me that Mrs Pinchbeck said that she had already telephoned for an ambulance but that since I was closer she thought that I would get there quicker.

Ermentrude and Theodore Pinchbeck live a few miles from Bilbury Grange, in a house on the edge of the nearby village of Combe Martin. Mr Pinchbeck, who once lived in a cottage in Bilbury, had been a patient of Dr Brownlow for some years. When he married and moved to Combe Martin, I happily agreed to continue to look after him and his wife.

Combe Martin is a fascinating village which has quite a reputation as a wonderful holiday resort but to be perfectly honest (and don't for heaven's sake tell anyone I said this) some people who go there feel rather let down; suspecting that the beauties of the place have perhaps been a trifle oversold and that the romance inherent in the name 'Combe Martin', is more attractive than the village itself. Personally, I like Combe Martin. It's a very quiet, gentle seaside village. But for those who go on holiday expecting funfairs, Punch and Judy shows, a promenade and donkeys it is probably something of a disappointment.

The village itself consists of just one long street (it is, according to proud locals, the longest street in England) and a rather small beach which, perhaps due to the idiosyncratic behaviour of local tides and winds, always seems to attract every piece of flotsam and jetsam going.

Combe Martin gets its name from the valley (the combe) in which it nestles, and from the Martin family.

The Martins (who originally spelt their names Martyn de Tours) were 12th century landowners and Lords of the Manor. They made a huge amount of money from farming and mining and spent some of their no doubt hard-earned loot on building a moated castle in the village.

The family died out when Robert Martin (or, to be more accurate, Robert Martyn de Tours), who was the last of the line, went out hunting early one morning. When it became dark and he still hadn't returned home, the servants raised the drawbridge, thinking that their master was spending the night elsewhere. They were accustomed to him staying away unexpectedly and probably assumed that, as was his well-known habit, he was busy besmirching the reputation of an unfortunate local maiden.

Sadly, however, there was no besmirching going on and when Robert galloped home, the moon was no bigger than a nail clipping and the sky was pitch black.

There is a strange and genuine blackness about moonless nights in the countryside. Even today, as a result of the fact that the village is miles from what city and town dwellers like to call civilisation, the night sky in Bilbury is far blacker than it is in urban and suburban areas.

Not seeing that the drawbridge was up, the hapless landowner rode straight into his own moat and drowned.

That was the end of the Martins but it was not the end of the village which became exceedingly prosperous from the 13th century onwards. There may not have been any Martins around but locals made a good deal of money from mining silver, iron and a pigment called umber; something which artists know well because when heated the colour becomes more intense and is known as burnt umber.

You wouldn't know it now but Combe Martin was once England's most important centre for silver mining and King Edward III, who was King of England for 50 years in the 14th century, pretty well paid the expenses of his war against the French with the silver dug from the Combe Martin mines. That was the war which Edward started when he declared himself to be the rightful heir to the French throne back in 1337. Things went well for a while, and Combe Martin's silver bought a number of notable and famous victories, but the war eventually turned into the Hundred Years War and when the Black Death plague hit England, the supply of men for England's army rather dried up and that was pretty well that for King Edward's plan to conquer France.

Sadly, although some mining continued until the early 20th century, the silver mining industry in North Devon pretty well died a permanent death in about 1830 when the inevitable happened and the silver ran out. Over the years, as the price of silver has risen, various attempts have been made to revive the mining industry but none of them has come to anything. All that remains now are some mine shafts and the ruins of a number of old mine buildings. There is a ruined engine house on Knap Down, on land belonging to Silver Mines Farm, and if you know where to look, and look hard enough, you can still see some signs of those now forgotten mines.

The Pinchbecks, my patients, live in a house which dates back to the 15th century and which had originally been built by one of the early mine owners. Like a good many old houses, it has been extended on numerous occasions since then and today it is, like so many buildings in North Devon, rather a mish mash of architectural styles. It is, however, a marvellous home with far reaching views over the coastline. On a clear day you can easily see Wales on the other side of the Severn Estuary.

Mr and Mrs Pinchbeck are a fascinating couple.

Mr Pinchbeck, who is in his late fifties and more than two decades older than his wife, has the earnest, naturally superior air of a butler, sommelier or a head waiter; an air of natural, condescending superiority mixed with a difficult to define awareness that his place in life isn't all that it is expected to appear to be. It isn't that officious, bullying, self-important superiority that typifies the more arrogant variety of police officer, the self-righteous customs official or the sneering tax inspector, but the quiet confidence, mixed with carefully modulated deference, that typifies the high ranking professional servant.

The odd thing is, however, that Mr Pinchbeck isn't a butler or a sommelier, though he does wear an old-fashioned frock coat and a carefully knotted white tie when he is at work. He is an old-fashioned dignified and respectful bank manager. He works in Barnstaple and can often be found standing in the foyer of his bank, greeting customers with a small bow and a few welcoming words. He exudes calm, dignity and respect and he is, generally speaking, the most ataraxic individual I know.

Mr Pinchbeck married late.

He was a confirmed bachelor who surprised everyone who thought they knew him by suddenly finding romance and a wife.

The odd thing is that they met each other on a Tube train in London. He was there to watch a cricket match at the Oval cricket ground. She was there to attend an educational conference. They literally bumped into each other, chatted and found that they both came from North Devon. They lived just a few miles apart but had to go to London to find each other.

Just before her marriage Mrs Pinchbeck (or Miss Kitchener as she was then) told me that she had read that, according to an old Devon saying, a bride should be half the age of her husband, plus seven years, if the marriage was to succeed. I remembered that I had heard the same saying credited to Corsica, Russia, Italy and, indeed, the whole of Victorian England, but I didn't mention this. She was a primary school teacher and, I suspected, a good one.

Today, Miss Pinchbeck is in her thirties and is a headmistress at a local school. I have to say that if I were one of her pupils I would be terrified – at first at any rate; unless or until I realised that the tough exterior hid a soft, gentle inner.

She rather reminds me of a gym master I had at school. His name was Sam and he was an ex-army instructor with a bark that had been honed on thousands of army recruits. He could snarl at a boy standing two hundred yards away and the boy would shiver with fear. But I realised one day that his bark was very superficial. A boy in my form slipped on a piece of equipment in the gym and hurt his thumb. Nothing was broken or dislocated and there was no sign of blood but the boy was close to tears. I suppose he had probably sprained it. Sam's response surprised us all. The man who had, moments before, been screaming abuse and telling us that he didn't care if we broke every bone in our bodies, was suddenly as upset and as sympathetic as the boy's mother could have been. He fussed over the mildly injured boy as though he had broken at least one major bone and personally insisted on escorting him to the school nurse.

That was Mrs Pinchbeck – as tough as a parking meter maid until or unless something went wrong. And then she became the kindest and sweetest and gentlest of souls.

She and her husband have two children, twins aged seven years.

When I arrived at their house, I found that I had beaten the ambulance but that the gardens looked like a battlefield. There seemed to be children everywhere. Some were screaming, some were crying and some were sitting on the grass rubbing their faces and rocking backwards and forwards in distress. Four adults, mothers and fathers I guessed, were standing around not sure what to do. The two mothers were crying. The fathers were clearly anxious to do something but clearly didn't have the faintest idea what the something should be. I spotted Mr Pinchbeck trying to talk to one of the mothers.

Now looking very forlorn, abandoned and out of place there were several trestle tables on the lawn. The tables were laden with half empty plates, empty jugs and trifle bowls that were pretty well empty. Whatever had happened had clearly happened after tea had been served. A dozen balloons were hanging from the branches of a couple of trees. Toys of various kinds were strewn about on the lawn. A small dog, a fox terrier, ran in and out, barking at anything and nothing. He didn't seem territorial or even particularly upset, and his tail was sticking as upright as a flagpole and wagging furiously. I got the feeling he knew he was really supposed to bark but that he couldn't really put his heart and soul into it because he knew something was seriously wrong but didn't understand what.

'It's the twins' birthday,' explained Mrs Pinchbeck, struggling to stay calm. She was wearing a pink summer dress and had her two daughters standing beside her. Both were crying. Both were cuddling their mother and clinging to her dress. One of the girls was hugging a large, beautiful doll with long blonde hair 'They invited a dozen or so of their friends round for a party.'

Mrs Pinchbeck was desperately upset and had to take deep breaths at the end of each sentence. With a nod and a murmur of encouragement, I waited for her to continue. I discovered long ago that it is dangerous to hurry into activity until you have an idea about what has happened. 'We let all the children go off into a field we own so that they could just run around and make as much noise as they wanted.'

'How long ago was this?' I asked.

'About an hour or so,' replied Mrs Pinchbeck. 'We first became aware that something was wrong about twenty minutes ago. I rang the ambulance and then I rang you. Thank you for coming so quickly.' She looked across the fields in front of the house. 'I don't know where the ambulance is.'

'They'll be here as soon as they can,' I assured her. 'They have to come from Barnstaple. I was only a couple of miles away. Can I speak to one of your daughters?'

I was pretty sure that I already knew what the problem was. It was something I'd seen before, but not on such a huge scale.

The small dog had now given up barking and was staring at me, with his tail still upright and still wagging. He seemed to want to play fetch or, failing that, to lie down in a nice cool spot and dream of rabbits. But he wanted me to decide for him.

'Chloe and Mathilda are here,' said Mrs Pinchbeck. 'Chloe doesn't seem too badly affected but Mathilda has nasty looking burns on her face, especially on and around her lips, and she has burns on her hands and arms.'

'May I look?' I asked Mathilda.

Slowly, reluctantly, she turned her face so that I could see the angry looking rash on her face. She then showed me her arms and hands.

I knew immediately that my guess had been an accurate one.

'You made some pea shooters?' I asked.

She looked surprised, but nodded.

'We found some plants with hollow stalks,' explained her sister. 'They made great pea shooters. I got some dried peas from the kitchen for the others. But I didn't play that game. I had my doll and my doll didn't want to play at pea shooters.'

'My guess is that there are some giant hogweed plants in your field,' I said to Mrs Pinchbeck. 'The plants look like cow parsley – but they're bigger.' Out of the corner of my eye, I saw the fox terrier wander off and start digging a hole in a flowerbed.

'There's quite a lot of what I thought was cow parsley,' agreed Mrs Pinchbeck. 'It's mostly around the edge of the field. But some of it is very tall – six or eight feet tall.'

She led me over to the field, just a few yards away from where I was standing. I could see that the edge of the field was studded with Giant Hogweed plants.

'Some of the plants are just cow parsley,' I said. 'But the taller plants are Giant Hogweed. You can deal with them another time. What we need to do straight away is to get all the affected children indoors, away from the sunshine, and into a darkened room. Then we need to wash their skin very gently with lots of soap and water to remove the irritant and to stop the burns getting any worse.'

I gathered together all the available adults and asked them to take the children into the house. Mrs Pinchbeck drew the curtains in the living room, to shut out as much light as possible, and the other parents started washing the children's skin. I gave antihistamines to the children to try to reduce the itching and the skin irritation.

'Are there any children with sore eyes?' I asked.

When I was assured that there were not I was hugely relieved. The sap of the Giant Hogweed plant can cause blindness. I went from child to child, checking their skin and making sure that everything possible was being done to minimise each child's symptoms.

'What on earth has caused all this?' asked Mr Pinchbeck. He sounded angry.

'The children cut up some Giant Hogweed stalks and used them as pea shooters,' I explained. 'The Giant Hogweed produces massively thick stalks which are hollow. Perfect for pea shooting.'

'What the devil is Giant Hogweed?' asked Mr Pinchbeck.

'It's a rather nasty plant which was brought to the United Kingdom by Victorian explorers who travelled to Southern Russia and Georgia – which is where the plant came from. They took seeds to Kew Gardens which then gave seeds to people who wanted the plant in their gardens. And since then it's just spread and spread, I'm afraid. The stalks have bristles on the stems and brushing against those can cause a skin reaction much like the sort of stinging you get from nettles. But it's the sap which really causes the problems. If the sap gets onto the skin and it is then exposed to the light, there is a reaction. It's a type of photodermatitis called phytophotodermatitis and it is caused by the fact that the sap sensitises the skin to both natural and artificial light.'

'Will it do any permanent harm?'

'They should all be fine in a day or two,' I said. 'Thank heavens none of their eyes are affected. That really is a miracle. We need to wash off all the sap and keep them all away from light for the rest of the day. I can prescribe some antihistamines which will help soothe the burning and it might help to apply some calamine lotion to the affected skin.'

Just then the ambulance came screaming into the garden. Considering how far he had to travel, along winding country lanes, the driver had made good time.

Three of the children were much more severely affected than the others, and although they probably didn't really need to go to hospital I decided that since the ambulance had arrived I'd take advantage of its presence to take those children to the hospital in Barnstaple. I telephoned one of the on-call doctors at the hospital and he agreed to take a look at the three worst affected children, and to keep them in for observation. He said there wasn't much he could do apart from give them antihistamines and an appropriate analgesic, but he had a few spare beds and agreed with me that keeping them for a while wouldn't do any harm. Neither he nor I thought they would need to stay in hospital for more than one night.

'Is there anything else we can do,' asked Mrs Pinchbeck.

'In a day or two you could put on some tough clothes and a pair of thick gloves and cut down the Giant Hogweed plants in your field,' I told her. 'Until you've done that I suggest that you keep the children out of the field.'

She said they would certainly do that.

I then drove home, at a rather more leisurely pace than I had driven to the Pinchbecks, and after I had enjoyed a nice cup of tea and a slice of Patsy's almond cake, I carried on cutting the grass.

And when I had finished cutting the grass, I wandered around the garden looking for Giant Hogweed plants.

I found at least a dozen of the damned things. And I chopped them all down before they could spread their seeds and create yet more plants.

British explorers brought all sorts of wonderful plants back to the United Kingdom. But occasionally we are, I think, entitled to curse their selections.

For example, I think it is fair to say that we would all be better off if the Giant Hogweed had been left where it was.

The Reluctant Winner of the Duck and Puddle Bowling for a Pig Competition

I don't know why or when the custom started but every year, without fail, Frank and Gilly at the Duck and Puddle organise a 'Bowling for a Pig' competition. A set of battered old, wooden ninepins are set up at the business end of the pub's skittle alley and contestants pay 20 new pence to roll three balls at the skittles. No one is allowed to have more than three goes (totalling 60 pence) and this is the only round of the competition for which a charge is made. All the proceeds from the event used to be shared between a group of national charities but recently the Bilbury Skittles Charitable Donations Committee (which is comprised of Frank and Gilly Parsons, the landlords of the Duck and Puddle) decreed that the proceeds from the event should in future be given to Bilbury's own cottage hospital (which is misnamed the Brownlow Country Hotel in order to avoid attracting the unwelcome attentions of local bureaucrats) in order that the citizens of Bilbury could benefit directly. Since the hospital spends no money on staff, marketing or advertising the Committee knows that every penny raised will be used to help patients.

Skittles is often confused with its modern successor, ten pin bowling, but the two games are really quite different – in style if nothing else. For one thing, there are nine skittles or 'men' and they are wooden. And after the skittles are knocked down, they are put back into position by hand.

One of the Duck and Puddle's skittles is noticeably skinnier and lighter than the others because in 1952, long before my time in Bilbury, a legendary farmer called Dick Westlake sent down a ball with such ferocity that the skittle which had taken the force of the throw split and lost a third of its size.

Over the years, the reputed size of Mr Westlake has steadily increased. He died in 1961 and was then generally reputed to be 6 foot 4 inches tall and to weigh 18 stones. But burying him didn't stop him growing. Today, if you ask anyone about Dick Westlake, they will tell you that he was at least 6 foot 10 inches tall and that he weighed 25 stones in his birthday suit and nigh on 30 stones with his boots on. He is said to have had hands bigger than a baseball catcher's mitt. When he was a young man, he spent some time in the army and they wanted him to be a boxer but, so the story goes, no one could find gloves big enough for his enormous hands. That was the man responsible for the fact that today the Duck and Puddle version of skittles involves eight and two thirds skittles, rather than the more usual nine.

The three balls, which, like the skittles, were hand carved from pieces of mature oak, were originally perfectly round and smooth but they too have, over the years, suffered rather a good deal from the battering they have taken.

The skittle alley, where the game is played, is protected on one side by a brick wall and on the other by a wooden fence which is two feet high and quite inadequate for the purpose. I have frequently suggested to Frank that he should at least double the height of the barrier in order to protect patrons from balls and skittles which bounce or ricochet over the fence and into the spectators. A couple of years ago, several spectators were injured (one with a fractured fibula and one with a fractured ulna) when an exceptionally enthusiastic but sadly wayward farm labourer from Codisworthy sent down a ball which not only missed all nine skittles but also missed the bowling alley and went sailing over the barriers into the crowd. Frank's argument, with which it is difficult to disagree, is that the wooden fence would have had to be ten foot high to have prevented such a wayward shot.

At the end of the skittle alley there is a wooden barrier in place, with sand filled sacks in front of it. The sacks are supposed to take the impetus out of the balls which miss the skittles and find their way through to the end of the alley.

The rules of the game are very simple.

Male competitors have to bowl their balls underarm and from behind a painted line which defines the start of the bowling alley.

Women have to bowl from behind a painted line which is a full yard closer to the skittles and they have the option of bowling underarm or overarm.

Male entrants have been banned from bowling overarm since Norman Tarragon, an assistant blacksmith, tried to get at two skittles which were the only ones of the nine which were still standing. The two remaining skittles stood behind the other seven skittles, which had fallen and which were lying in front, making a very effective barrier. Tarragon bowled an overarm donkey drop which missed the target by six feet, went through a closed window, damaged two cars and a bicycle and somehow ended up just two or three feet away from the village pond.

My concern, that any one of the numerous spectators standing watching could well have been seriously injured, was dismissed as irrelevant and scaremongering namby pamby nonsense but there had been genuine concern that the misdirected ball could well have been lost forever if it had sunk into the mud around the edge of the pond. It was this fear, not any concern for the wellbeing of contestants or spectators, which had led the Duck and Puddle Skittles Rules Committee (a rather grand name for Frank and Gilly) to announce that in future male bowlers would be deemed to have bowled illegally, and disqualified from the competition, if they bowled overarm. This had produced some muttering among the older villagers but when it was pointed out that it would be pretty well impossible to find a carpenter capable of carving a perfectly round replacement ball which matched the size and weight of the other two, the dissent disappeared.

The other rules are very simple.

Everyone who succeeds in knocking down all nine skittles with their three balls goes through to the second round of the competition and their names are inscribed, by Gilly, on an old blackboard which had, several years earlier, been retired by our village school. When all the competitors have had their maximum possible three attempts, the second round begins. No fees are charged for this or for subsequent rounds. Contestants are allowed only one attempt to knock down all the skittles with their three balls. Successful entrants then go through to the third round and so on and so forth. Eventually, there will usually come a point where there are just two or three contestants left in the competition. This, since it is the final stage of the competition, is known as the Final Round.

At this point in the competition, Frank announces that the Final Round has commenced and it is customary for the remaining

16

contestants to have a break to take refreshment. Traditionally this consists of a packet of pork scratchings and two pints of best bitter, though in 1963, a man who was both a vegetarian and a teetotaller reached the final and Frank temporarily amended the unofficial rules so that he was allowed to take a packet of salt and vinegar crisps and two pints of tonic water and lime.

(Frank said afterwards that anyone who can down two pints of tonic water and lime deserves all the luck he can get and that the rest of us should get behind him and give him our support. Sadly, however, the teetotal vegetarian, clearly suffering from an ailment known to sheep farmers as the bloat, failed to progress any further in the competition.)

The Finals are run in exactly the same way as the other rounds.

Each remaining player attempts to knock down the nine skittles with the three wooden balls. Any player who fails to do this is eliminated from the competition.

Usually, the competition finishes between midnight and one am and Frank, as licensee of the Duck and Puddle, always applies for, and is always given, an official extension to his opening hours.

Occasionally, the competition continues for longer and when this happens Frank usually gives himself permission to keep the bar open until he deems it necessary to close it.

On one famous occasion, Thumper Robinson and Jack Rattenbury were locked in competition until 6.35 a.m. on the morning after the event had started. The excitement was so great that very few, if any, of the spectators left the sporting arena. With a pub full of eager customers Frank, who is if nothing else an independent man, would no more think of throwing the towel over the pumps than he would think of putting prawn cocktail and Black Forest gateau on the Duck and Puddle menu. Thumper eventually won the pig that year. It was the first of his three victories.

Three years ago a German tourist and his wife, who were on a touring holiday of the West Country, took part in the competition and in honour of their attendance, Frank and Gilly decided that the event would in future be known as the European Skittle Bowling for a Pig Championships.

And, in the year of which I write, when two American tourists arrived, hot foot from Idaho, and the male half of the partnership declared that he would be competing, the competition was renamed the Official World Skittle Bowling for a Pig Championships. Never let it be said that we in Bilbury do not know how to take full advantage of a situation.

The two Americans, Edgar and Delphinium Rathbone, had never visited England before and they were determined to try every experience available. And there is no doubt that their adventures were certainly giving them much to write home about.

On the day of their arrival, they had both gone fishing for trout in the river Lynn at Lynmouth. They had hired Thumper Robinson as their guide. Neither of them had ever been fishing before and when Edgar, keen to emulate Thumper's expert cast and full to the brim with false confidence and genuine enthusiasm, took his rod back a little too far, the result was that the hook and fly went through an open window in one of the terraced cottages overlooking the river, and caught on a piece of curtain. Thumper said he had been very impressed because although he had been fishing many times (sometimes with a rod and sometimes with his bare hands, for he was a skilled trout tickler) he had never before seen anyone catch a terraced cottage. He said he was pretty confident that it was the heaviest catch any fisherman had ever hooked.

The prize for the winner of what must now surely be Bilbury's premier sporting event is, as might well be surmised when folk hear the name of the competition, a pig.

But, unlike other similar 'Bowling for a Pig' competitions around the country, the pig on offer is not a mere piglet; some hardly visible creature weighing no more than a puppy; a delicate creature which can be picked up and cuddled. The prize is always a proper, fully-grown male porcine adult; a fully signed up comrade of the genus Sus, and a neatly defined member of the Suidae family of even toed ungulates. In Bilbury, as Frank once said, we do not like to do things by halves. If there is to be bowling for a pig then the prize will be a pig – and not a piglet.

And throughout the event, the pig at the heart of the proceedings, the star of the evening, invariably grunting and snuffling with undisguised delight, lies comfortably in a corner of the room wherein lies the skittle alley, and had munched his way through an armful of mixed carrots, turnips and potatoes.

On this occasion a small sign, attached to the wall where the pig lay, informed observers that his name was Cedric.

Naturally, not all the winners of the skittle competition have either the accommodation or the temperament required to care for a fully-grown pig who fully intends to carry on growing.

First and foremost, of course, an adult pig requires a solid, well-made sty, something constructed with rather more concrete than wood. And he needs a bit of land around the sty so that he can roll in the mud, snuffle around for roots and other tasty comestibles, and lie in the sunshine when the fancy takes him. It is, perhaps, not widely known but pigs like to loll around in the sun doing nothing, just as much as they enjoy a good meal. The pig sty itself needs to provide shelter from the elements and plenty of fresh straw bedding and the attached land should enable the pig to do a little occasional exercise and a little quiet daydreaming.

And second, there is the food.

Pigs do not grow to the size they generally become by nibbling an occasional lettuce leaf and they do not maintain their generous proportions by nibbling on low calorie biscuits and sipping designer water through a straw. They do not stint themselves when dining. They are gourmands rather than gourmets and for them it is quantity rather than mere quality which determines their happiness. Finding enough food to keep a pig content requires a strong back, determination, a truck of some kind and a never-ending supply of suitable comestibles. Expecting to make do with an occasional slop bucket full of household waste will simply not do. Day in, day out the pig must be fed and, in the absence of a ready supply of pigswill from a school canteen, will require a vast supply of cereals, potatoes, carrots and other vegetables. Feeding a pig can be an exhausting and expensive business.

And what, in the end, do you do with your pig when you have fed it for a year or two and its size has increased in a satisfying manner to a fairly healthy 200 to 250 pounds?

The obvious answer, of course, is to turn the pig into a freezer full of pork chops and rashers of bacon. A decent sized porker will provide enough nourishment to last a large family some months; providing its executioners with two dressed sides, two hams, two shoulders, ribs with meat attached, blade bones, backbone with meat attached, head and tongue, trotters, tail, liver, kidney and heart and a seemingly inexhaustible supply of bits and pieces which veterinarians know as lungs, stomach, intestines and bladder and which butchers refer to as offal. Even when I ate meat I couldn't bear eating offal.

But, as quite a number of winners of the Duck and Puddle Bowling for a Pig competition have found, it is not easy to call in the slaughterman when you have got to know your animal and have found yourself smiling and nodding wisely as you lean on its gate and observe its little ways.

It is especially difficult to bring the animal's life to a sudden end when you have given him or her a name.

It is much easier to order the death of 'the pig in the end sty' than it is to tell the man from the abattoir to pop along and kill Cedric.

The fact is that pigs are intelligent animals and they all have individual skills, peculiarities, eccentricities and idiosyncrasies of their own.

If a census were taken in Bilbury today, and pigs were included in the population, the pigs would comprise a healthy, sizeable ethnic minority. And if all those pigs were given the vote, and there are many pig owners who will tell you that their pig is more intelligent than many of the people they know, and certainly more intelligent than the majority of politicians, then there are those in the village who would say that the world would be a better place. There would be fewer wars and far more rooting for vegetables, and who will argue that would not make the world a better place?

Bilburians are generous, warm-hearted, broad-minded, welcoming people and if someone in London wants to give pigs the vote then we'll be the first to go along with it, and welcome pigs and sows into the electoral community. Still, I can't see it happening any time soon.

Bowling wooden balls at skittles is not, I think it is fair to say, an activity which requires a great deal of thought, or even a good deal of skill. It does require a certain amount of brawn, for the balls are heavy and must be projected with some force if they are to knock down the skittles, rather than simply rest wearily up against them; but not many would regard nine pins (its other name) as requiring the same level of mental agility as, say, chess or dominoes. A darts player is required to do a little rudimentary mathematics from time to time but all the skittles player has to do with his brain is count the number of skittles which are still standing, and then act accordingly.

Of course, as with any game, there are players who claim to have acquired special skills. There are some skittles players who take pride in their ability to knock down a solitary wooden man who is guarded by eight fallen comrades. Such a shot requires the ability to throw a 'beamer' or a 'bouncer'. A 'beamer' is a ball which does not land on the wooden planks which make up the base of the bowling alley but travels straight from the player's hand to the target. A 'bouncer' is a ball which lands but once, and then leaps forwards after bouncing. Some players claim to be able to put spin on the ball (a skill which requires hands the size of hams and fingers strong enough to bend nails) and others claim that they can fire a ball at the skittles at a speed of 30 to 40 miles per hour.

But much of this is harmless phooey, and those who have been watching skittles for some decades will confirm that the one ingredient which really matters, and the one which all players require above all else, is good old-fashioned luck.

When Edgar Rathbone from Idaho became the surprise winner of the latest Duck and Puddle competition, there was much delight and a good deal of excitement. Mr Rathbone was not only the first winner from the United States, he was only the second winner who did not hail from Bilbury or one of the nearby villages.

'We're truly global now,' said Frank, positively purring with delight.

Peter Marshall wanted to know if Mr Rathbone thought there might be a market for old-fashioned skittle alleys in Idaho. He explained that he could provide any interested parties with a full inventory of equipment, including skittles and balls. (None of us who heard this sales pitch could imagine where Peter could possibly find wooden skittles and balls.)

Mr Rathbone, who seemed rather surprised by this suggestion, said he felt sure that there would be a market for such a 'quaint, old-fashioned sporting activity'. I really liked the Rathbones. They were a kind couple, always eager to please and always keen to see the England that the English know. He had, I think, been something big in motor car sales. She had managed a drugstore.

Many questions were asked from those who wondered precisely how Mr Rathbone intended to deal with his success. And the obvious question (no less pertinent for it being so obvious) was: 'Are you going to keep the pig and, if so, how are you going to get him back home to Idaho?'

Mr Rathbone's wife, Delphinium, who had become quite pale when she realised that her husband had won a pig, wanted to know if they really had to accept the prize or if there was, perhaps, an alternative option. 'A box of chocolates?' she inquired hopefully. 'Maybe a bottle of your lovely British sherry? Or a box of assorted, coloured bath salts?'

On reflection, I suppose it must have been quite a shock for both of them.

Most visitors touring England are happy to pick up the usual souvenirs; items which will fit comfortably into a suitcase: a few photographs, a handful of postcards, an assortment of English stamps, a box of shortbread or chocolates, a small toy model of a red London bus, a small bust of Shakespeare, a London theatre programme – that sort of thing.

Not many tourists suddenly find themselves to be the rather shocked owners of a large pig.

The Rathbones were travelling around the West of England in a rented Ford Capri and had found themselves in Bilbury, staying at the Duck and Puddle, simply because they had got lost while trying to drive between the twin Devon villages of Lynton and Lynmouth, and the small town of Bideford further along the coast.

The fact is that if you get lost in Bilbury there is nowhere else to stay other than the village's one hostelry. The choice is simple: a room at the Duck and Puddle or park your car in a field gateway.

And now, with absolutely no warning, the two travellers had become three.

Mr Rathbone had forked out his entry fee for no other reason than that he thought it would be something truly Devonian to talk about when they got back home. Delphinium had taken several photographs of Edgar posing with one of the wooden balls. It had not occurred to either of them that their modest investment might produce such an unexpected dividend.

You can see that under such circumstances any sensible woman might well prefer finding room in her suitcase for a box of bath salts to continuing her journey around the West Country with a 200 pound carrot munching machine lying on the back seat of your rented Capri

– especially when you and your husband have signed a document promising to return the car in a 'clean condition'.

The Rathbones were both in their 60s, and it is fair to say that they were keen and experienced travellers.

They had visited Europe on a dozen occasions and they had enjoyed or endured the usual variety of adventures which befall travellers in Europe. They had been held up at customs posts, they had filled in endless forms, they had stood patiently as their suitcases had been examined in minute detail, they had stayed in hotels where the plumbing had been considered primitive in 1920 and in France they had endured the discomfort of the Turkish lavatory – an item of plumbing known in Turkey as the Indian toilet and one which requires the user to squat rather than to sit.

But they had always managed to complete their travels without ever once acquiring a pig as a travelling companion.

At first, thrilled by his unexpected success and sustained by enthusiasm rather than practicalities, Mr Rathbone said that they were experienced in the care of animals. However, he admitted, when asked, that their knowledge of animals was confined to having, over several decades, shared their home with one Persian cat and two consecutive Bichon frise dogs. In addition, Mr Rathbone remembered that he had been the owner of a goldfish early in his life, though he readily agreed with those observers who felt that, with all due respect, the goldfish,(Mr Rathbone thought it had been won at a fair of some kind), being a creature which required little more than a pinch of feed and an occasional change of water, could almost certainly be disregarded and dismissed as providing negligible practical experience in the handling and transport of fully grown adult members of the family suidae, part of the order artiodactyla.

The truth is that, however you look at things, winning a pig is some way removed from winning a goldfish in a glass bowl or owning a cat that looks good sitting on the sofa. The domestic pig is, after all, closely related to the hippopotamus. The Rathbones, it was generally agreed, had no relevant experience for the job of looking after an animal weighing 20 stones, having a mind of its own and requiring a good deal of attention.

'How would we get it in the car?' asked Mrs Rathbone. 'Does he answer to his name? Where will we find a collar and lead big enough? Do hotels and pubs in England provide accommodation for people travelling with pigs?'

And, of course, the inevitable query: 'Is he house trained?'

It was generally agreed that it would be impossible to get Cedric into anything smaller than a truck, that hotels in England do not usually provide special accommodation for travellers arriving with pigs, that it would be difficult to find a suitably sized collar and lead and that Cedric was definitely, quite definitely, not house trained. The straw upon which Cedric lay provided ample evidence of this shortcoming. It is an inevitability that when you put a good deal of something into one end of a pig, a good deal of something else will eventually come out of the other end.

The Rathbones whispered quietly and rather urgently to each other and then Mr Rathbone approached me.

'Do you have a farm, doctor?' he asked.

I told him that Patsy and I had a smallholding and a fair amount of land but that we didn't have what anyone could call a proper farm.

'But you've got stables and things?'

'Oh yes,' I said, 'we've got stables and outbuildings.'

Mr Rathbone lowered his voice. 'I'm very honoured to have won the pig,' he said, 'but Delphinium and I are a bit worried about exactly what we're going to do with it.' Delphinium, who was standing just behind her husband, nodded and took her husband's hand.

'Even if we managed to get it back to the States where would we keep it?' asked Mrs Rathbone. 'We live in a condominium. All we've got outside is an allocated parking space.'

'We wondered if you would take the pig,' said Mr Rathbone.

'Sort of just look after it for us,' said Mrs Rathbone.

'We don't want her turning into sausages,' said Mr Rathbone. 'We'll pay for the food and the upkeep,' he added.

'Perhaps you'd send us photos occasionally, let us know how she's doing,' said Mrs Rathbone.

'He, dear,' said Mr Rathbone gently. 'Cedric is a 'he'.'

'Oh yes,' said Mrs Rathbone. 'Let us know how he's doing.'

I looked at Patsy. She smiled. She didn't actually nod but I knew her well enough to know that she was nodding in her mind.

'We'll be delighted to take him,' I said. 'And we'll happily send you photographs. But we don't want you to send us money.'

'We'll be thrilled to look after Cedric,' said Patsy. 'You must come to the house tomorrow,' she looked at her watch, 'well, later today. And we'll show you where she's going to be living. I'll ask my dad to pick her up in his trailer tomorrow morning. If you come round later in the morning you'll be able to see her settling in. And you must stay for lunch.'

The Rathbones were delighted, grateful and very relieved. They made serious attempts to persuade us to let them send us money to buy turnips and carrots but, when we made it clear that we didn't want them to pay anything but were happy to have the opportunity to look after their pig, they gave in gracefully. The truth is, we told them, was that we were both rather proud to add a very fine looking pig to our small menagerie. 'He'll be a member of the family,' Patsy assured them. 'And he'll never be turned into sausages or rashers of bacon.'

The Rathbones who were, of course, staying at the Duck and Puddle went upstairs to their room and Patsy and I headed for the door.

Most people had gone and the bar was pretty well empty. Patsy and I had both enjoyed a splendid evening, all the more so for the fact that it was a rare treat for us. We could not go out together very often because either Patsy or I usually had to be at Bilbury Grange in order to answer the phone in case of an emergency. If I was not there, Patsy had to be available to tell anyone who turned up on the doorstep where I could be found.

And so we usually had to have our days out separately. Once or twice a week, Patsy would have an afternoon or an evening out (usually with her sister Adrienne) and once or twice a week, on evenings when she wasn't going out, I would potter along to the Duck and Puddle for an hour or two playing bar billiards or darts, invariably with my chums Thumper Robinson and Patchy Fogg. If there was an emergency of any kind Patsy would ring me at the pub and Frank would give me the message.

On special occasions, such as the evening of the skittles competition, Patsy's parents would babysit the little ones, answer the telephone if it rang and tell callers where I was. They would then spend the night in our spare room.

Patsy and I were half way through the door, ready to head for home when Gilly suddenly came running up to us.

'It's Frank,' she said.

Gilly is usually calm; a rock in the rough seas which are an inevitable part of life when you are married to Frank and when you share with him the responsibility of running a village pub.

I had never seen such terror in her eyes.

Patsy and I both stopped.

'What's wrong with him?' I asked her. I had drunk a couple of glasses of whisky but suddenly I was cold, stone sober.

'I think he's had a stroke,' said Gilly.

And suddenly, completely unexpectedly, entirely understandably, she burst into tears.

Frank's Stroke

I was shocked, saddened and desperately worried but not terribly surprised to hear that Frank had suffered a stroke.

Frank Parsons, the joint owner and sole licensee at the Duck and Puddle, has had high blood pressure for some time and he has constantly refused to listen to my requests for him to change his lifestyle.

He weighs too much, he eats too much (and eats a good deal of fatty food such as chips and pies), he drinks too much alcohol and he smokes too many cigars. He has maturity onset (type II) diabetes but he persistently refuses to follow any of the dietary advice I give him. He takes almost no exercise at all (a trip down into the cellar to connect up another barrel of beer, or to hunt out a special bottle of wine, have been his only exercise for several years) and although he likes to think of himself as tough and resilient he is, in reality, a sensitive man who worries far more than he allows the wider world to suspect.

He is also, as he himself is fond of saying, 'not as young as he was when he wasn't as old as he is now'.

In short, Frank has, for some years now, been a medical accident waiting to happen.

His only concession to my pleadings (and to those of his wife Gilly) has been to give up the cigarettes he has smoked since he was 14-years-old and to replace them with cigars.

I have told him that there is no evidence that cigars are safer than cigarettes but he says they must be doing him much less harm because he only smokes five or six cigars a day whereas he used to smoke fifty or sixty cigarettes a day.

I pointed out that the Churchillian sized cigars which he smokes contain far more tobacco than ten cigarettes but talking to the cigars would have had just as much effect.

All this went through my mind in a flash as Patsy and I followed Gilly.

Frank was lying on the floor at the bottom of the winding and narrow staircase which leads up to the bedrooms and down to the cellar in the Duck and Puddle. Oddly, and with extraordinary good fortune, Frank had collapsed more or less in the recovery position. He was unconscious and he had vomited.

'At first I thought he'd fallen down the stairs,' said Gilly, 'but when I looked at his face I could see that he'd had a stroke.' She had made a real effort and had stopped crying. I turned and quietly asked Patsy, who had her arm around Gilly, to use the pub's telephone to call an ambulance.

'Have you moved him?' I asked Gilly, checking Frank's pulse and breathing. The publican's pulse was a little fast but it was regular. His breathing wasn't good but at least he was breathing and his colour wasn't bad. I checked his mouth to make sure that there wasn't any vomit blocking his airway. There wasn't.

Gilly shook her head. 'He's too heavy,' she said. Gilly weighs probably a third of Frank's twenty stone.

'That's good.'

I knew that although Frank had definitely had a stroke it was perfectly possible that he'd also fallen down the stairs.' I started to check him over as I spoke and was relieved that I could find no sign that any bones were broken.

'I think he'd just come up from the cellar,' said Gilly. 'He said he was going down to fetch another bottle of port for a nightcap.' She pointed to a bottle lying, unbroken, on the floor. 'The port is there so he'd probably just made it to the top of the stairs when he collapsed.'

'He hasn't injured himself,' I said, when I'd finished checking him over. 'I can't find any signs of any broken bones – though it's perfectly possible he may have cracked a rib or two of course. He probably fell quite heavily.'

Frank, who was now starting to regain consciousness, mumbled something incomprehensible. I leant down and listened carefully.

He repeated what he'd said and this time I worked out that he was telling us that he hadn't fallen but had suddenly felt his right leg give way.

'You've had a stroke,' I told him, 'but you're going to be fine. We have to get you into hospital in Barnstaple but we'll soon have you home.'

Slowly, Frank moved his left hand to his forehead and held it in the way that people tend to do when they've got a bad headache.

'Do you have a headache?' I asked him.

He said something but I couldn't understand him. His speech was definitely affected; and affected quite badly. I leant closer and repeated the question. This time I could make out the answer. 'Yes'.

Obeying the instinctive, irresistible urge to comfort someone by touching them, I put a hand on Frank's shoulder. It may sound hard hearted to say so but knowing that Frank had a headache provided another clue to help make an accurate diagnosis. But I couldn't give him anything for the headache until I had a better idea of what had caused the stroke.

Frank said something else.

After he'd said it the third time I realised that he was asking for Dr Brownlow.

I tested the muscles in his right hand and then those in his left hand. His right hand was limp and without power. His left hand was fine. The stroke had definitely affected the right side of his body.

A stroke usually develops because of a problem with the blood supply to the brain and there are three principle types of stroke.

First, there is the stroke which develops because a blood clot forms at a particular site within the brain, blocking the oxygen supply to the brain cells. Second, there is the stroke which develops because a blood clot which has formed elsewhere in the body travels, as an embolism, and causes a blockage, blocking the oxygen supply to the brain cells. Third, there is the stroke which develops because there has been a bleed within the brain. This is known as an intra-cerebral haemorrhage and this sort of stroke is often a result of high blood pressure.

Around four fifths of all strokes are caused by a clot blocking an artery and thereby depriving brain cells of their regular and essential supplies of oxygen and glucose. The damage done by a clot can vary enormously from person to person. Some people can have quite a large clot in their brain but show very few symptoms while others, with exactly the same sort of blockage, may have signs of a massive ischaemic stroke. Why this happens is something of a mystery but it is probably because of the presence or absence of collateral arteries which, when present, can protect patients from the consequences of a stroke. An individual who has large collateral arteries (which can provide a secondary blood supply to an area of the brain theoretically deprived of oxygen by a clot) will suffer far less than an individual who has small collateral arteries. It's all down to the luck of the draw.

The other thing that affects the amount of damage that is done by a blood clot in the brain, is the length of time the brain cells go without blood. If they are deprived of blood, and therefore oxygen and sugar, for a brief time then the brain cells may recover completely. But if the brain cells are deprived for longer, some of them will die and some brain function will be lost. That's the bad news. The good news is that it is sometimes possible for another part of the brain to learn to do the things that the damaged cells can no longer do. Doctors and nurses are constantly working at finding new ways to help stroke patients recover lost skills.

There is another type of bleeding which can cause a stroke and this, called a subarachnoid haemorrhage, occurs when a blood vessel bursts within the subarachnoid space which surrounds the brain. This type of bleed usually results from a weakness in an artery wall called an aneurysm and it mainly affects younger people.

Those are the main types of stroke caused by blood vessel problems.

Strokes can also develop if there is a tumour in the brain but knowing a good deal about his medical history, I was prepared to guess that Frank's stroke wasn't caused by the sudden appearance of a brain tumour.

Besides, if Frank's stroke was caused by a tumour then there wasn't anything much I could do to help him immediately. But if his stroke was caused by an intra-cerebral haemorrhage or an embolism then there were things I could do that would prove beneficial.

The worst type of stroke is usually the one caused by bleeding within the brain. This is the type of stroke which most commonly causes sudden death. And, whereas with a clot in the brain the damage tends not to get any worse, with a bleed things can continue to deteriorate for some time after the onset of the first symptoms. The longer the bleeding continues the worse the symptoms will be – and the greater the problem.

A clot will usually block off an artery to a particular part of the brain. And that, God willing, will be that. Unless there are several clots the damage will be done when the clot arrives at its destination.

But once bleeding starts within the brain it can go on and on. The damaged area can continue to grow.

The odd thing is that whether the stroke is caused by a clot or a bleed, most of the immediate symptoms will be pretty much the same.

An area of the brain is deprived of oxygen and the result can be a mixture of physical and mental symptoms. Patients may lose the control of certain muscles (usually on the opposite side of the body to the side of the brain where the brain occurred) and they may sustain problems with their speech, their memory and their intellect. It is common for stroke victims to be emotionally labile too, and to become frustrated because they cannot think clearly.

The truth is that, in my experience, virtually anything can happen after a stroke – none of it likely to be on anyone's Christmas list.

Although I had no way of knowing what had caused Frank's stroke, I was prepared to guess that it was related to his blood pressure. And when high blood pressure causes a stroke, there is a good chance that it will be a stroke caused by bleeding inside the brain.

I took a firm hold of Frank's right hand. His speech was so badly affected that I needed to establish another way to communicate with him.

'Squeeze my fingers if you understand me,' I told him. 'Squeeze once for 'yes' and twice for 'no.'

He squeezed my fingers once. His grip in his good hand was as strong as ever.

'Dr Brownlow isn't here,' I told him. 'But I'm looking after you.' I told him my name. 'Do you remember me?'

One squeeze.

Frank tried to say something else. He was trying desperately to say something but the words were just not coming out properly. I listened carefully and suddenly realised what he was trying to say to me.

'The Dr Brownlow Hospital? You want to go to the Dr Brownlow Hospital?'

I understood at last. From Frank's point of view it made complete sense.

We don't actually, officially, have an official hospital in Bilbury. But we have a sort of hospital.

My late hero, friend and mentor, Dr Brownlow understood just how bad hospitals had become. He spent his final weeks at home, being cared for by his faithful butler Bradshaw and he wanted his permanent legacy to be a small, friendly hospital run by people who genuinely cared about the sick and the weak and the frail. He left his home, and a good sum of money, so that we would be able to create a cottage hospital that would provide the villagers of Bilbury with a haven and a refuge at their time of need.

Up until Dr Brownlow's generous gesture, Bilbury had never had a hospital of its own and villagers who needed nursing care or palliative care, had always had to go into hospital in Barnstaple or Exeter. Most, if not all villagers, disliked this idea very much. Their relatives and friends all lived in Bilbury and it's quite a trek from the village to Barnstaple. People who had to rely on public transport found the journey next to impossible. There are no trains, of course, and buses are as rare as apples on pear trees. It's a well-known fact that people who fall ill abroad always want to be cared for at home. And the people of Bilbury were no different: if they had to be poorly then they'd rather be poorly in Bilbury than anywhere else. If they needed to have an operation, or to undergo extensive tests and investigations, they would grit their teeth and go into a large hospital in a large town. But if they just needed to be looked after then they would, all things being equal, prefer to be looked after in Bilbury.

After Dr Brownlow died I appointed his former butler, Bradshaw, as my district nurse but I also decided that he would be the only person suitable to take on the responsibility as the matron of the new cottage hospital. Bradshaw found enough volunteers to staff the hospital without our having to hire any professional nurses. Most of the volunteers had no academic nursing qualifications but they all had a quality which is far more important than any number of diplomas: they were all intrinsically kind people.

Our plans to provide Bilbury with its own small hospital did not go completely according to plan, of course.

Local health service administrators were obstructive and it quickly became apparent that converting Dr Brownlow's home into a hospital was going to be far more difficult than we had thought. As soon as we had solved one problem, the red tape loving pen pushers thought of another problem.

It was Bradshaw who pointed out that we didn't need our hospital to be registered as an 'official' hospital' and it was Bradshaw who suggested that instead of calling our establishment the Bilbury Cottage Hospital we should call it the Brownlow Country Hotel, and run it, officially, as a hotel. And so we refer to our patients as 'guests' and the health service people have no authority over us.

Instead of being matron at the Brownlow Cottage Hospital the incomparable Bradshaw became the manager of the Brownlow Country Hotel.

And that was where Frank wanted to go.

The publican squeezed my right hand firmly. Once. I could tell by the look in his eyes that he was desperate to go into our local hospital – and not one of the big, super-efficient hospitals. I realised that this was probably what he had been trying to tell me when I thought that he had asked for Dr Brownlow.

'The ambulance is on its way,' murmured Patsy, who had come back from the telephone.

'Is Frank going to be all right?' asked Gilly.

'Frank is going to be fine,' I told her. 'He's had a stroke affecting the right side of his body so we know that the problem lies in the left side of his brain. His right arm and right leg aren't working properly and his speech has been affected. But he can hear us and understand us.'

'Is he going to be paralysed?' asked Gilly. 'I just want to know. I'll look after him whatever has happened. I just want to know. I need to know the worst.' She started to cry again. 'He's not going to die, is he?'

'He's going to be fine,' I told her, with far more confidence than I could possibly feel. 'The paralysis is temporary. And he is definitely not going to die.'

I didn't know this, of course. To be perfectly honest, Gilly could have answered that question as well as I could. But I needed her to be as calm as possible. And, most important of all, I needed Frank to be relaxed and calm. If he became agitated then his blood pressure would soar and if the stroke had been caused by bleeding then the size of the bleed within his brain would grow and the problems would get worse.

The more I thought about it the more I became convinced that Frank's stroke had been caused by a bleed.

With Frank listening to us, and conscious of every word I spoke, it was particularly vital that I did everything I could to ensure that he remained positive and calm. And I needed Gilly to be alert and able to think clearly. This was not a time for worrying or for gloominess.

I took the keys to the boot of the old Rolls out of my jacket pocket and handed them to Gilly. 'My black medical bag is in the boot of the car,' I told her, 'would you fetch it for me, please? I'd like to check Frank's blood pressure.'

I never bother to lock the car doors in Bilbury, but if I'm leaving the car for any length of time I always put my drug bag into the boot and lock the boot lid.

I realised just how lucky it was that I had the car with me. Patsy and I had originally decided to walk from Bilbury Grange to the Duck and Puddle but we had, in the end, decided to take the car because Patsy was wearing a long dress and her one pair of really high heels. The lane which leads from our house to the pub is used by several farms and the animals, cows and sheep, which are herded along the lane are generous in making sticky deposits upon the rutted and potholed tarmacadam.

Frank spoke again. I looked at him. He repeated what he had said. I listened carefully. There was a desperation in his eyes.

'You don't want to go to the hospital in Barnstaple?'

I was still holding his hand he squeezed my fingers very tightly. Once. He didn't want to go to the hospital in Barnstaple. Indeed, it was clear that he was becoming very agitated at the thought that he might be taken to Barnstaple.

I understood why.

'You don't want to go to the hospital in Exeter?' It is important when asking questions this way to make sure that they can be answered with a simple 'yes' or 'no' answer.

Another single squeeze of my fingers. Another 'yes' from Frank.

To those of us who live in Bilbury, the town of Barnstaple is almost another world. It is a place with banks and offices and traffic lights and pavements. It is a town where locals can walk down the street and not recognise one in ten of the people they see. And the hospital is a large, unfriendly building. There are the usual seemingly endless corridors, the awful décor, the usual smells and the inevitable feeling, for both patients and visitors, of being trapped in some Kafkaesque nightmare. It isn't the fault of the staff. It is just the way too many large modern hospitals seem to be.

But I knew that there was something else; another reason why Frank was desperate not to go to the hospital in Barnstaple or the one in Exeter.

Both of Frank's parents had died in the hospital in Exeter and Frank had always thought that the deaths had been unnecessary. Frank's father had died of an infection which he had acquired in the hospital and his mother had been misdiagnosed and mistreated. We had talked about both deaths on numerous occasions and I confess that I had agreed with his suspicions.

I understood why Frank wanted me to take him into our local cottage hospital. But I really didn't think the Bilbury hospital was the right place for a patient who had just suffered from a stroke.

We have had several stroke victims in our village hospital but they were all patients who had been seen in either the Barnstaple hospital or the Exeter hospital and whose condition had been fully diagnosed. They had come to the hospital in Bilbury for rehabilitation; to be nursed and to be helped to learn again how to use their muscles and their minds. We had all the basic nursing equipment we would need, including a hoist to help move heavy patients in and out of bed, but we didn't have any sophisticated, diagnostic equipment.

I had a terribly difficult decision to make.

The treatment of a stroke depends, inevitably, upon the cause of the stroke. And it isn't easy to decide what did cause a stroke. Hospital doctors have equipment and laboratories to help them make diagnoses.

I knew that if I asked the ambulance crew to take Frank to Barnstaple or Exeter, the doctors there would be able to examine him far more thoroughly than I ever could. They could do tests that I couldn't do. And then, after a week or so, we could have him transferred back to the hospital in Bilbury. That was the logical, sensible thing to do.

But I knew that Frank was terribly worried about going to one of the big Devon hospitals. I strongly suspected that if he did go to the hospital in Barnstaple, or to the one in Exeter, the result would be that his blood pressure would soar. And the journey alone wouldn't be much fun for a frightened and partly paralysed man. It would take the ambulance a good three quarters of an hour to reach Barnstaple and longer to get to Exeter; moreover all the roads along which the ambulance would have to travel are winding and poorly kept, with surfaces which have, in many places, been damaged by frost and are, therefore, marked with more than a few potholes.

All that was bad enough.

But my real worry was that Frank would be so upset at the very idea of going to a big hospital that his blood pressure would go up and up.

And if his blood pressure rose then there would be a greatly increased chance that the stroke would get worse.

If the stroke got worse then there was a considerable chance that Frank would die.

Making decisions about the care of patients is always difficult. But when the patient concerned is a close friend, that decision becomes even more difficult. In a large practice I would have been able to call in another partner, and ask for his or her advice and help – particularly for a patient whom I knew so well. But in Bilbury, in a single-handed medical practice, I was on my own. I had no one to ask for advice.

Suddenly, unbidden, I recalled the first time I met Frank.

I had arrived in Barnstaple, clutching my medical bag and a blue cardboard suitcase, and when I stepped from the train to the platform, the first thing I saw was a small crowd gathered around a fat man in a tweed suit, gaiters and heavy brown boots. The man on the ground was lying flat on his back. It was Frank. He had been to a Licensed Victuallers Association meeting in Exeter and he was stone cold drunk. I remember travelling with him to Bilbury, in a taxi driven by Peter Marshall.

I remembered Frank, slightly recovered, climbing out of the taxi and standing, wobbling slightly, while Gilly, his wife, told him what she thought of him.

I remembered, in a flash of disconnected sequences, the hours I had spent in Frank's company. I remembered the times when I had tried, quite unsuccessfully, to persuade him to lose a little weight and at least cut down his smoking. I remembered laughing when he had drawn the pub curtains on a sunny day because he complained that the sound the sunbeams made as they bounced upon the furniture was making his head hurt. I remembered laughing with him,

Thumper and Patchy as we tried to play darts blindfolded. And then by facing the wrong direction and throwing the darts over our shoulders. I knew the holes which our darts had made in the wall were still there.

Frank had been a central part of my life for so long that I could not imagine a world without him. When he laughed properly it was a real belly laugh. It sounded like thunder.

I remembered that he and Gilly had occasional huge rows. She once locked him out of the Duck and Puddle and told him to sleep in the shed. I offered him a bed for the night but he wouldn't take it because he said that if Gilly thought he needed to be taught a lesson then she was right and he needed to be taught a lesson. They had huge rows but they always made up soon afterwards. I remembered the two of them, with their arms around each other: a genuinely loving couple.

I remembered the days when financial problems meant that the two of them nearly lost the pub. I remembered Frank's endless generosity and his unbidden, natural kindness.

All this I remembered in a single flash.

Gilly returned with my medical bag. She handed my keys and I unlocked the bag. It is, not unreasonably, the law that a doctor must keep any dangerous drugs, such as morphine, double locked. And so I kept my locked bag in the locked boot of my car.

But it wasn't drugs I needed from my bag.

I took out my sphygmomanometer, rolled up Frank's shirt sleeve and took his blood pressure.

It was 220/160. Even for Frank this was high; frighteningly high.

Since he was my patient, and I had taken his blood pressure many times, I knew that his blood pressure was normally around 160/100. That is high enough to need treatment but if I could somehow get Frank's blood pressure down to that sort of level, I would be very happy.

A normal, young adult will have a blood pressure of 120/80. The two numbers, known as the systolic and the diastolic figures, mark the highest and lowest pressure created as the heart pumps blood around the body.

If it weren't under pressure, the blood in the human body wouldn't go anywhere. It would just lie around in arteries and veins doing no one any good at all. Tissues would receive no oxygen or glucose, and waste products would accumulate. Before long everything would die. But when the blood pressure rises too high then the danger is that a blood vessel will burst and blood will leak out. When the blood vessel which bursts is in the brain then the individual concerned will have a stroke. If the leak is a very small one then the chances are that the stroke will be a mild one. But if the leak is a big one then the stroke can be massive or fatal. The more I thought about it the more I was convinced that this was what had happened to Frank.

I guessed that the stress and the excitement of the 'Bowling for a Pig' competition had pushed Frank's blood pressure way up into dangerous levels. Frank is the sort of old-fashioned landlord who likes to see his customers having a good time. And throughout the evening he had been constantly rushing around trying to make sure that everyone present was having a good time. He had probably drunk more alcohol than usual too. And for Frank a normal evening of drinking would probably put most of us under the table.

'What's his blood pressure like?' asked Gilly, who was kneeling beside me on the floor.

'It's a little on the high side,' I told her. I didn't think of it as a lie but as a tactical understatement.

'I made some coffee,' said Patsy. She handed me a cup and gave one to Gilly too. I took the cup, thanked Patsy, and sipped while I thought. I didn't need sobering up, the emergency had done that quite adequately. But the hot coffee was welcome. My mind was racing as I tried to decide what I should do with Frank. Should I risk sending him to Barnstaple? Should I send him to Exeter? Or should I risk keeping him in Bilbury, at a local cottage hospital with nice clean sheets, nice beds and pretty well no medical equipment more sophisticated than a thermometer.

It was, without a doubt, the most difficult decision of my career. I knew that if I got it wrong then Frank would probably die.

And, as an irrelevant aside, I could end up being struck off the medical register for making the wrong decision. I would be in a tricky spot if Frank died and I was asked to explain why I had chosen to send him not to a hospital but to a place officially registered as a country hotel.

There was absolutely no doubt that from a perfectly selfish point of view I had no choice: I had to send Frank into the hospital in

Barnstaple and hope that the long, uncomfortable journey didn't kill him and that the stress of being in a place he feared didn't push his blood pressure into the stratosphere.

I checked his arms and his legs as best as I could. The paralysis caused by the stroke did not appear to have increased

I knew that the first thing I needed to decide was what had caused Frank's stroke. Was I right to guess that his high blood pressure had caused a bleed? Or could the stroke have been caused by a clot?

Statistically the odds were that the stroke had been caused by a clot. I told myself for the tenth time that four out of five strokes are caused by clots rather than bleeds.

The fact is that the basic symptoms of all types of stroke are similar (a loss of motor function and a loss of various mental functions such as speech, sight and so on) but there are some signs and symptoms which can help differentiate between the two types of stroke.

And when I stopped and thought about I realised that I really had all the information I needed to make the diagnosis. I already knew which side of his brain was affected. All I had to do was to decide whether the problem was a clot or a bleed. That decision would decide what needed to be done next.

If Frank had suffered a clot in his brain then he needed to be started on anticoagulants to break up the clot. If he had suffered a bleed because of high blood pressure then it was essential to lower his blood pressure.

On the other hand, if he had suffered a bleed and I, or any other doctor, gave him anticoagulants then the bleed would get worse and he would almost certainly die.

I sipped the coffee which Patsy had made while I thought about the facts I had available. I knew that if the patient had been a stranger I would have found everything so much simpler.

I tried to sort through all the evidence I had which might help me make a diagnosis.

There are some differences in the two main types of stroke, the bleed and the clot. Patients who have had a stroke caused by a bleed may have some symptoms which aren't common among patients who have had a clot.

My mind raced as I tried to think back and assess every piece of information I had gleaned. I needed to make a decision before the ambulance arrived in order to know whether to tell the ambulance crew to take Frank to one of the big hospitals or to the Brownlow Country Hotel here in Bilbury.

Patients who have had strokes caused by bleeds rather than by clots are more likely to lose consciousness immediately after their stroke. It is also commoner for patients who have had strokes caused by bleeding to have a severe headache. And it is commoner for patients who have had strokes caused by a bleed, rather than a clot, to feel nauseous or to vomit.

Frank had lost consciousness, he had a headache and he had vomited.

All those symptoms suggested that my guess was correct: that Frank's stroke was caused by a bleed.

And, one other thing, he had very high blood pressure.

It is very high blood pressure which commonly results in a stroke caused by a bleed. High blood pressure can rupture a blood vessel and cause bleeding but it isn't as likely to be a factor in the production of a blood clot.

I turned to Patsy. 'How many patients do we have in the Bilbury hospital?' I asked her.

The official name for the Bilbury hospital may be the Brownlow Country Hotel but I always think of the place as the Bilbury hospital. And that's how we usually refer to it.

She looked at me and frowned. 'You're not thinking…'

For the first time Patsy realised that I was thinking of keeping Frank in Bilbury, and looking after him myself. She knew how difficult a decision it would be. And she knew that if I got the decision wrong then Frank could die. She'd been a doctor's wife long enough to know that it is almost impossible to make decisions like this accurately without doing sophisticated hospital tests. And she'd been my wife long enough to know how much I would be worrying about the decision.

'How many?' I asked her again. I knew damned well how many patients we had in the local hospital but I didn't have enough brain left to find the answer from my own memory.

The Brownlow Country Hotel only has one professional nurse. We can call on several voluntary workers, some of whom have a little nursing experience, but the only nurse is Dr Brownlow's old butler, Bradshaw, who is officially also my district nurse.

Bradshaw lives at the Brownlow Country Hotel and although he is in his 80s (he has been in his 80s for as long as I can remember) you wouldn't think it if you saw him rushing around. He may have a Christian name but no one ever uses it. He always has been, is, and probably always will be just 'Bradshaw'.

'Just two,' Patsy replied. 'Miss Havistock and Mrs Pettigrew.'

I knew them both well, of course.

Miss Havistock was in her eighties and frail. But she was alert and she was in the Brownlow Country Hotel only because her small cottage was being decorated after a flood in her loft had brought down the ceiling in her bedroom. Mrs Pettigrew was slightly younger and was there because she had been in hospital in Exeter having a hip replacement operation. She was just about ready to go home and required very little nursing care.

All this was important because if I decided to take Frank into the Bilbury hospital then he would need a good deal of nursing care. We would have to make sure that he didn't stay immobilised for too long, that if he was in bed for long periods then he was turned regularly so that pressure sores did not develop, that he was kept properly hydrated, that his blood pressure was brought down and under control. And we needed to keep a careful eye on him to make sure that the stroke wasn't getting worse. I would need to examine him thoroughly, muscle by muscle, so that I knew exactly which parts of his body had been affected. Only if I knew what was affected now would I be able to tell if the stroke was getting worse. If it was getting worse then that would mean that the bleed was continuing and if that happened then we would need to rush him to a major hospital for surgery. If an artery continues to bleed, and just won't stop, then it is sometimes necessary for a neurosurgeon to go into the brain and tie off the artery causing the trouble.

Both Miss Havistock and Mrs Pettigrew could pretty well look after themselves. In fact, I suspected that having them there would be a help. Both would happily help with looking after Frank, even if that just meant taking it in turns to sit by his bedside, keeping an eye on him and being prepared to call Bradshaw or myself if we were needed. In big hospitals they have machines which beep and have blinking lights to tell the nurses and doctors when something goes wrong. We had no such machines in Bilbury.

Just thinking about all the problems made me feel dizzy, and nearly convinced me to do the safe thing and send Frank to Barnstaple. Or maybe to Exeter. The Exeter hospital is bigger and better equipped than the one in Barnstaple. I knew that there were neurosurgeons working there. Maybe if I were to send Frank into one of the big hospitals I should try to arrange to send him to Exeter.

But I resisted the fears, mine and Frank's, and tried to be entirely rational.

I still believed that Frank's best chance was to stay in Bilbury and to be looked after in the Bilbury hospital.

I had, just a week or two earlier read research papers which showed that patients who are kept at home after having suffered heart attacks have just as good a survival rate as patients who are admitted to Coronary Care Units or Intensive Care Units. The problem is, it seems, that a hospital environment can be so terrifying that many patients suffer a relapse, or fail to recover, because of the intense stress they feel. Hospital units which are set up to deal with emergency patients tend to be full of bright lights and beeping machinery. Nurses are forever moving about, checking on this and checking on that. There is no privacy, no quiet, no peace and no chance for a patient to sleep. And so patients who can be kept at home, and looked after quietly in the peace of their own environment, where they feel safe and comfortable, will often do just as well, or even better, than patients who are taken into hospital, connected up to electronic machinery and drip bottles and given vast quantities of medication. This is the case for heart attack patients. But was it also the case for patients who had suffered strokes?

I had left the cuff wrapped around Frank's arm. I took his blood pressure again. It was 200/150. It had come down a little since I had last taken it. That was good news. I checked his limbs again. There had not been any deterioration; the paralysis did not seem to be any worse. If I was correct in thinking that Frank had suffered a bleed and not a clot then the bleed had stopped and Frank's condition had, for the moment at least, stabilised.

Suddenly, I made the decision.

'I'm going to take you into the local hospital,' I told Frank. 'You will do as you are told. You will not smoke any cigarettes. You will not smoke any cigars. You will not smoke a pipe. You will not drink any alcohol. No gin, no beer, no whisky, no wine – no alcohol at all.

You will eat what you are told to eat. And you will damned well get better. Do you understand?'

Frank turned his head slightly, looked at me and tried to smile.

'OK,' he said. I heard it clearly.

I looked up to Patsy. 'Ring Bradshaw,' I told her. 'Tell him to get up and get dressed and get ready to receive a patient.' I paused. 'You can tell him who it is.'

I then looked at Gilly. 'I'm keeping Frank in Bilbury because I think I know what's caused his stroke and I think we can deal with it best here. He'll be agitated and stressed and his blood pressure will soar if I send him to Barnstaple.'

'Thank you,' murmured Gilly.

'But he and you have to do what I tell you,' I said. 'He will want you to smuggle in fags and booze. You will be tempted. But if he smokes or drinks alcohol then he will die and there will be nothing I or anyone else can do for him.'

I was deliberately trying to frighten Gilly because I knew that this was probably the best chance I had to make her realise just how important it was that she listened to me and took me seriously. Frank can be persuasive and charming and Gilly adores him. I knew that if Frank asked Gilly to take him a packet of cigarettes or a bottle of whisky she would be tempted.

Suddenly, we could all hear a siren approaching.

The ambulance was on its way and I knew that for many of us in Bilbury life was going to be very different for quite a while.

And I had taken a decision that could, I knew, change all our lives.

A Rather Busy Day

Patsy and I settled Frank into our small local hospital and by the time we got back to Bilbury Grange it was nearly three in the morning. We were both exhausted. Gilly, having helped settle Frank into bed at the hospital, had gone back to the Duck and Puddle where the Rathbones had long since gone to bed. I had given Bradshaw instructions to check Frank's blood pressure regularly and to call me immediately if it went up at all. Bradshaw, who sometimes struck me as having superhuman qualities, seemed perfectly capable of going for days without sleep. Patsy's parents, our babysitters, had gone to bed in our spare room.

Patsy and I crept into the children's bedroom and said goodnight to them. We then undressed, washed without much enthusiasm, and clambered into bed. When I last looked at the alarm clock by our bed it showed ten to four in the morning.

The next time I saw the clock it was five o'clock. I had been awakened by the telephone. It was still a good two and a half hours earlier than my usual start to the day.

The caller was the wife of a patient of mine called Gardner Hoskins, who had only been out of hospital for three days. His wife had rung, in an entirely understandable panic, to tell me that Gardner was complaining of severe abdominal pain. I told her that I would be there as soon as I could, leapt out of bed, pulled on my trousers and a jumper which I always keep by the side of the bed so that I can dress quickly when I have a night call, and was in the car no more than five minutes after I had woken. My black medical bag was already back in the boot of the car.

The Hoskins live in a small cob walled cottage a few miles away from Bilbury Grange and by the time I got there I was pretty sure that I knew exactly what had happened. After one brief look at Mr Hoskins, I borrowed the telephone and rang for an ambulance. When I'd done that I rang the hospital, spoke to the house surgeon on call and told him that I was sending one of his patients back to him. Not surprisingly, he didn't sound too excited. Hospital doctors who send patients home, like them to stay at home rather than come whizzing back like an unwelcome boomerang.

I told the house surgeon that they would probably have to do some repair work to the stitching on Mr Hoskins's large bowel. That pleased him even less because he knew he would have to telephone the surgical registrar and maybe even the surgical consultant. The chances of either of them being happy to be awoken were slightly slimmer than nil.

Mr Hoskins had been diagnosed with bowel cancer, and a surgeon in Exeter Hospital had removed the growth and pronounced himself satisfied that he had managed to remove all of the tumour. Tests on samples from Mr Hoskins's lymph glands had shown that there had been no spread and the surgeon had told everyone concerned that he was well pleased. Mr Hoskins had an excellent prognosis. We had all been delighted.

But now the patient was lying flat on his back and he was clearly in a good deal of pain. He was as white as the proverbial sheet and he was soaked with sweat. I reached out and touched his abdomen. It was as rigid as a board.

I guessed what had happened because standing on the bedside table there was a large bottle of a well-known fizzy drink; one widely promoted as being suitable for the sick and the convalescent.

'How much of that stuff has he been drinking?' I asked his wife.

She looked puzzled but thought for a while. 'I think he drank two bottles yesterday,' she said. 'But the nurses at the hospital said that he had to have plenty to drink.'

'But preferably not anything fizzy,' I told her.

'What's happened?' asked Mrs Hoskins.

'The gas in that fizzy drink has blown up your husband's bowel and burst the stitches,' I explained. 'As a result of that, some of the bowel contents have escaped into his abdomen. And your husband now has peritonitis.'

'Is it serious?' she asked, whispering.

'It will be if we don't get him straight back into the hospital,' I told her. 'I've asked the ambulance people to get here as fast as they can. And as soon as your husband arrives at the hospital they'll start treatment with an antibiotic. That should help clear up the infection.

If I'm right they will then have to go back into your husband's abdomen to repair the stitching to the large bowel.'

'Will he be all right?' she wanted to know.

'He'll be fine,' I told her.

I then waited with her for the ambulance to arrive. And after he had gone off back to Exeter I drove back to Bilbury Grange.

On my way home I had to pass St Damian's, a small Grade I listed 12th century church which, technically at least, stands just outside the village boundary but which is still regarded by many older villagers as the holiest of all the churches in Devon. From the outside, the church remains in pretty much the same state as it must have looked in the 12th century. It has a small, stubby tower but has never had a spire attached.

Saint Damian was a Catholic saint who was the twin brother of Saint Cosmas. I bet there aren't many twin brothers who are both saints. The pair of them, both of whom were physicians who practised in what was, at the time, a Roman province of Syria, were Christian martyrs. They practised their profession for free, making their skills and knowledge available to anyone and everyone. Today the twins are regarded as the patron saints of all doctors and surgeons though, I'm sad to say, there are a good many doctors and surgeons who have never even heard of them.

Curiously, and inexplicably, there are very few churches in England dedicated to the memory of either twin.

I had, I realised, to my shame and regret never once been inside St Damian's. Neither Patsy nor I are regular churchgoers. I once explained to a clergyman that we both considered ourselves to be irreligious Christians and he understood what I meant.

I'm not sure why I noticed the church or felt the need to stop and go inside that morning. But I stopped the car, parked it on a stretch of verge, and tried the door of the church. To my delight the huge oak portal, decorated with huge iron straps and hinges, swung open with great ease. Grinning gargoyles, their likenesses doubtless based on the masons who had built the church, stared down at me; welcoming the honest in spirit and frightening off the evil.

Once inside, I spent a few moments exploring the church. Curiously, as is often the case with some old buildings, it seemed bigger when I got inside than it looked from the outside. There was a

46

row of musicians' stalls and there were some box pews which looked as if they had probably been added in the 18th century. The pulpit looked Georgian and there was a clerk's stall and a reading desk for the minister. A huge impressive wooden screen, which I guessed probably dated from the 18th century, had inscribed upon it the Lord's Prayer and the Ten Commandments. There was a life sized wooden statue of St Damian which was carved in oak and which had, I suspected, probably been there as long as the church had been standing. I guessed that very little about the church had been changed in the centuries it had been standing.

I opened the small wooden door to one of the pews and knelt on a hand-embroidered kneeler. At that moment I knew why I was there; understood why I had entered the church. And I began to pray.

I prayed for Frank; asking whoever might be listening to help him recover his physical and mental strength. And, I prayed that I had made the right decision in keeping him in Bilbury and not telling the ambulance crew to take him to a major hospital. In my heart and mind I still felt that I had made the right decision. But I knew that if it turned out that I had made the wrong decision then I would struggle to cope with the guilt I would feel. And there would, I suspected, be many outside the village who would be quick to point a finger and criticise. In the cold light of day, and with a chance to reflect, discuss, share and assess all the consequences, it is often much easier to make a decision. From a personal point of view, the sensible decision would have been to pass Frank's care onto the doctors at the hospital in Barnstaple. No one could have ever blamed me for making that decision. I suddenly remembered, incongruously, that someone had once told me that no one in business, given the task of buying a computer for his firm, had ever been fired for buying an IBM machine. I was reminded of this because I doubt if any doctor has ever been disciplined or pilloried for sending a patient to the nearest large hospital. It is the default decision.

After I had prayed I stayed, kneeling and silent, for a few minutes more. I thanked God for helping me find Bilbury and for giving me a family which filled my life with joy and pride. I thanked Him for the work he had provided for me and I thanked Him for the friends I had found in Devon.

When I got back home, there was little point in going back to bed so I made myself an early breakfast.

47

I sat outside, with my breakfast on a garden table, and fed the birds and the squirrels and I sang them silly songs, made up as I went along. The garden creatures were all surprised to be fed so early but none of them seemed to mind in the slightest. I enjoy feeding the birds enormously and sometimes lose track of time when I'm out in the garden. Apart from my 'singing', and that of the birds, there was nothing whatsoever to be heard. Indoors, you could have probably heard the sound of dust settling.

One of the joys of living in the countryside is the fact that it is so quiet. No horns tooting, no pneumatic drills, no bus engines, no shouting. The last time I was in a city, I was shocked at the amount of noise – and its very persistence. It seemed to me that many of those who were out and about early in the morning were deliberately trying to make as much noise as they possibly could; perhaps because they hated the idea that the citizens who were still in bed might be enjoying a few minutes more abed than they themselves had enjoyed. The rubbish collectors, in particular, seemed to obtain particular pleasure from banging and shouting far more than seemed entirely necessary.

The star of the morning feeding is invariably the arrival of Percy. He pecks at the dining room window if he hasn't been fed and tends to wander around the garden behind me if I go for a walk. He is so tame that he invariably comes running when I call his name. He is easily recognisable because he has a grey patch amidst the green on the side of his neck, one of his tail feathers is missing and he limps noticeably because he has a bad foot; one of his toes is missing though I don't know why.

The funny thing is that he is the third generation of pheasants who have been coming to have breakfast with us. His grandfather first visited a few years ago and then when he found a wife and had a family he brought them along to introduce them. Possibly, I suspect, because he was rightly proud of them all. The female pheasant lays around a dozen eggs but neither parent takes much care of them, so to have two healthy daughters and a healthy son was not bad going.

Then when his son of the original Percy had his own family, he too brought along his wife, his two daughters and his son.

We call them all Lord Percival, shortened to Percy. I don't know why, we just do.

Percy, the grandson and the third generation, wasn't there this morning and I missed him. I could not remember the last time he hadn't come running when I had called him.

There's a surprising amount of mystery about pheasants. No one ever seems to really know what they eat. Some say they eat grain, others say that they prefer insects and some say they eat whatever seeds they can find, from dandelions and so on. In my experience, pheasants are probably the most omnivorous of birds; eating pretty much whatever is available – even mice if they're particularly peckish. Our Percy will eat peanuts and loves raisins but his preferred breakfast is a handful of sunflower hearts.

I couldn't help worrying about him.

The pheasant is a large bird but he is prey to a good many predators; with man, of course, being at the very top of the list. Pheasants are desperately easy to catch for poachers. They usually roost off the ground (Percy has a favourite branch over our lake) and, strangely, they prefer to run rather than fly away when threatened.

I was still worrying about Percy, hoping at any moment to see him running across the lawn in his slightly, almost comically, uncomfortable way, when Patsy, in her dressing gown, called to tell me that I had a telephone call from the hospital.

When I got to the telephone, I found that the house surgeon at the hospital had rung to tell me that the consultant surgeon had decided that my diagnosis was absolutely accurate. Moreover, X-rays had confirmed our diagnosis. The hospital doctors had started a course of antibiotics and, the young house surgeon told me, would be taking Mr Hoskins back to surgery to repair the broken stitches.

As soon as that call had finished I telephoned Mrs Hoskins and told her the good news. 'He'll need to stay in a hospital for a few more days,' I told her. 'But he'll be home soon.'

I told her to make sure that she didn't give her husband any more fizzy drinks.

And then it was time for the morning surgery.

There were twelve patients that morning and most of them were suffering from fairly straightforward problems.

We'd enjoyed a couple of days of good weather after a terrible few weeks and it seemed that half of the inhabitants of Bilbury had been out in their gardens; cutting grass, pruning overgrown bushes (there's no point in waiting until the autumn to do the pruning when your garden gate has disappeared under a cascade of hazel bush branches) and pulling up weeds. The majority of my patients had muscle strains as a result of doing too much, too quickly and with too much enthusiasm. One or two also had stings (wasp and nettle) and few odd cuts and lacerations.

The rest of the morning surgery included three people who'd acquired summer colds, one who had a bad gash on his arm which he had repaired, surprisingly successfully, with duct tape ('Didn't like to bother you on a Sunday, doctor', he said, though knowing a little of his reputation I rather suspected that there might have been another reason for his failure to take time out to telephone me or to call at the surgery) and two who simply needed to have their blood pressure checked (both needed to have their medication reduced slightly since the warmer weather often results in a lower blood pressure and a risk of hypotension).

The man who had gashed his arm and then rather artfully taped it together with a length of grey duct tape, is a local character called Albert Rhodes (who is usually known to those in the village as 'Icy' unless he owes them money in which case he is known as 'Slippery').

When I first moved to North Devon I thought that a man who was known as a 'character' would probably be just that: someone who smoked a curvy, Sherlock Holmes pipe and wore a tweed deerstalker hat or a fellow who had swum the Sargasso sea and climbed Mount Everest with his leg in a brace. Or, perhaps, someone like the novelist Patrician Highsmith, who kept snails in her handbag and would feed them lettuce when she was out for the evening. Someone like that.

But I was wrong, of course.

In Bilbury, and indeed throughout North Devon, a man who is known as a 'character' is almost always something of a crook. Saying that someone is a 'character' means that you have to keep your hand on your wallet and count the wheels on your car when he's gone.

'How did you get this?' I asked, as I sewed up Mr Rhodes's arm, hoping that my neat stitching wouldn't interfere too much with his tattoo of a four-masted schooner. I couldn't help noticing that he smelt of something cheap and foul. It was, I suddenly realised in silent horror, the same cheap aftershave that I spray onto our rubbish bags so that the foxes and badgers won't tear them open. I suppose I should have been honoured. 'Icy' had obviously sprayed himself with something rather pungent in order to disguise more natural odours. Like courtiers a few centuries ago, he found spraying on perfume easier and quicker than bathing. Sadly, whenever I smell that stuff I think of rubbish bags. Icy isn't the first of my patients to favour this particularly pungent aromatic.

'Just caught my arm on a bit of barbed wire,' he answered without hesitation. I knew he was lying. A barbed wire cut always seems to have a unique appearance, showing both the entry point and the signs of an attempted disentanglement. This was definitely not a cut made by barbed wire, razor wire or any other type of wire. This was a cut caused by a knife. Mr Rhodes had been stabbed.

When he'd taken off his shirt I'd seen the scars of pellet marks on his back and one or two wounds which could have easily been the result of previous knife fights. I remembered that I'd treated Mr Rhodes on several previous occasions when he had come to see me showing signs that he may have come off second best in some sort of confrontation.

'Are you sure this was barbed wire?' I asked him, peering at the wound. 'I need to know what caused the wound if I'm going to treat it successfully.'

There was a long, long pause. 'It might have been a knife,' he admitted, after some hesitation.

I guessed that he had probably lied because he didn't want me to report him to the police. Mr Rhodes was a poacher and a petty thief. I suspected that he had probably been selling stolen stuff to a fence and had found himself in a knife fight.

'I'm not going to report you to the police or anyone else,' I assured him. 'Have I ever reported you in the past?'

I remembered now that he had twice come to see me to have shotgun pellets removed from his back and his bottom. He knew damned well that I had never reported him, or anyone else, to the police

He shook his head and then looked at me for a while, weighing me up, before nodding. 'It was a knife,' he admitted. Although he trusted me more than most doctors he was, nevertheless, still rather cautious.

51

I know that the medical establishment and the police believe that doctors have a duty to report any suspicious wounds to the authorities but I also know that I am the only doctor for miles around and if I get a reputation for dobbing in my patients then people will simply refuse to come to see me. I was pretty certain that Mr Rhodes had obtained his wound some distance from Bilbury but had been reluctant to visit a hospital or local doctor lest he find himself answering questions from a policeman. He had waited until he got back to Bilbury because he knew that I would treat him with proper reverence for the Hippocratic Oath and the principles of confidentiality. The rules for country doctors have to be rather different to the rules for city based doctors and hospital doctors. I need my patients to trust me always; and to know that whatever they tell me or show me will be kept confidential. Without trust my job would be impossible. If doctors break the Hippocratic Oath of confidentiality then they don't really have much left. And if I, as a country doctor, didn't respect my patients' privacy they wouldn't come and see me at all. And if they didn't see me then they probably wouldn't see anyone.

I cleaned the wound, put in six or seven stitches, gave him a couple of injections and then wrote out a prescription for an antibiotic. 'Come and see me in a couple of days,' I told him.

'To have the stitches taken out?' he asked.

'No, no, the stitches will need to be in for longer than that. I just want to make sure that the wound isn't infected.'

He nodded, put his shirt back on and then touched his forehead with the index finger of his right hand in a gesture of respect. 'Grateful to you, doctor,' he said. 'You're a reliable fellow for a man of learning.'

I took the compliment with a nod of my own and reminded him to come back and see me in 48 hours. I don't like or trust poachers or thieves in general and I don't much like Mr Rhodes in particular but my job is to try to mend him and keep him alive rather than to pass moral judgement on his behaviour.

After Mr Rhodes had gone, right at the end of the surgery, just as I felt certain that I was nearly finished for the morning, Mr Mole appeared; Gerald Lancaster Mole to give him his full name.

'I waited until you'd seen everyone else,' he said, as he sat down with a sigh. There was a long pause during which he adjusted the razor sharp crease in his trousers. It was a long time since I'd seen a local inhabitant with a deliberate crease in his trousers. Most of my patients have creased trousers but the creases have been earned rather than delivered by the manufacturer. Mr Mole sighed again. 'I don't think you're going to be able to solve my problem in a few minutes.'

My heart sank. I already felt as though I had done a full day's work and I knew that I had three patients requiring home visits.

I saw from his medical notes that Mr Mole was 65-years-old. His birthday had been just six weeks earlier and so he had officially been a pensioner for precisely that long. I wondered if he was having a bit of crisis. The midlife crisis is well known, and often written about, but there are, of course, other times in our lives when we find ourselves facing, and having to deal with, psychological problems as we go through age milestones.

So, for example, many people find retirement difficult to cope with because it is so clearly a defining point in life. For most people their life's work is over, and the arrival of the first pension cheque is a clear sign that the last days of autumn are finished and the potentially harsh, uncomfortable days of winter have arrived. People who held important jobs, and who felt useful at least and important at best, will suddenly find that they are no longer powerful or significant.

'When I got to the age of 63 I thought I would build a wall around the garden,' said Mr Mole. 'I knew I only had a couple of years to go before I reached retirement age and I thought that if I started the wall before I retired, and built up my bricklaying skills, it would be something to do in my twilight years. I've never been a man for sport, not a golfer or a tennis player or a hiker, and I've never seen the point in collecting things, stamps, books and so on. I find television provides a thoroughly unsatisfying diet of unremitting pabulum. Nevertheless, like a lot of people I know I spent much of my life looking forward to the day when I would retire; the day when I wouldn't have to put on the suit and tie, catch the train and plod my way through the City with the rest of the lemmings. But the closer my retirement came the more I began to worry about what I'd do with the rest of my life. I didn't say anything to my wife, she worked as a librarian and retired at 55 and now she works in a charity shop three days a week, but I threw myself into building my wall and to be honest I think I became a bit obsessed. I spent all my evenings and weekends working on it.'

'My wife and I have always kept ourselves to ourselves and she's always been happy to stay at home, watching television and doing her knitting. She's very keen on knitting. I have more jumpers and cardigans than I could possibly wear out and a lot of the stuff she knits they sell in the charity shop where she works.'

Mr Mole took out a pen and started to fiddle with the top. 'We've never been ones for having an active social life,' he said, and then stopped as though thinking about this. He put the pen away and pulled out a linen handkerchief which he started to twist between his fingers. 'I told myself that I was doing the bricklaying because I wanted a nice wall around the garden, something to give us privacy, but eventually I realised that wasn't the case at all – the building of the wall was a goal in itself.'

'I've seen it,' I told him, 'it's a very splendid wall. You can be proud of it.'

'Oh I am, I am. But now that I've finished the wall my life seems totally without purpose. I built my wall too damned quickly and now I have nothing left to do. My working life was over when I retired and now the only really engaging hobby I've ever had is over too.' He looked straight at me. 'It seems strange to realise that my life is now pretty well over. I'm still alive, still here, still breathing, but that's about it.' He sighed, put away the handkerchief and took out the pen again. He sat and thought for a while. I didn't say anything. Sometimes, people need time to think through what they want to say.

'The funny thing is that my life just sort of happened,' he said at last. 'I never planned anything. I admire those people who set off at the age of 20 with plans for their whole lives. They set themselves targets and then they set off along the route they've designed for themselves. I never managed to do any of that. Everything that has happened to me has happened more or less by accident.'

'I think that's probably much the same for a lot of people,' I told him. 'It's certainly true for me. Serendipity rules OK?'

He smiled and we sat in silence for a few moments; both of us immersed in our memories.

'I can't keep building walls around the garden, can I?'

I smiled but didn't say anything.

'I don't suppose you want any walls building, doctor?' He was smiling and I don't think it was a serious question but I answered it nevertheless.

I shook my head, rather sadly. 'I'm afraid we have all the walls we want,' I told him. 'We're pretty well satisfied as far as walls are concerned.'

'I suppose I feel a bit depressed, really,' said Mr Mole. 'Have you come across this sort of problem before, doctor?'

I told him it was really very common. 'And it's not just retired folk who feel as though their lives have come to an abrupt and uncomfortable halt,' I pointed out, explaining that it is not at all uncommon for people of any age who have worked hard on some particular project to feel depressed and empty when the project is completed. Even students who have studied for an examination may feel strangely unhappy when the exam is over and the concentrated period of study is finished. Explorers who have spent months or years preparing for a particular expedition will often feel enormously sad when the expedition is over – however successful it may have been, and however painful and arduous the exploration. When we throw ourselves into something then it is inevitable that the conclusion should leave us empty in some strange, almost indefinable way. I told him that it has been said that 'when Alexander saw the breadth of his domain he wept for there were no more lands to conquer'.

I told Mr Mole that he had done the right thing by finding himself a project, the building of his massive garden wall, into which he could put his body, mind and spirit when his day to day work was done. But, sadly, he had thrown himself into the project with such commitment that he had finished the wall at about the same time as he had retired – leaving himself doubly unemployed and empty.

I told him that I could give him pills to help smother the sense of sadness he felt but that they would make no long-term difference. 'When you stop the pills the chances are that the sad feeling you have now will come back. You will have simply delayed the moment when you have to come face to face with your sense of emptiness.'

'So, what do I do?' asked Mr Mole.

'That's easy,' I told him, 'you have to find something new to fill your life. Maybe not a wall to build, but something that provides you with a real challenge. Make a list of all the things you are interested in, the things you like doing, the things you've always wanted to do but have never had the time to try.'

'I'm too old to try anything new,' said Mr Mole, rather sadly.

'Nonsense!' I said, firmly. 'People much older than you are have done astonishing things with their later years.'

I told him that if he would make the list I had suggested then I would think hard about his problem and put together a list of people who had done great things in their sixties and beyond. I told him to come back and see me later that same evening.

And so that afternoon, after I'd finished the home visits and had called to see how Frank was getting on in our local hospital, I spent an hour or two searching through the reference books in my library and creating a list of all the astonishing things people had done after the age of 65. Frank had not been looking too bad at all. His blood pressure had come down a little more and there had been no deterioration in his condition. Bradshaw thought he was definitely looking better.

It wasn't too difficult an exercise for I have managed to put together quite a decent reference library. Many of the books were left to me by Dr Brownlow, my predecessor and mentor, who had collected together an impressive library. Some of the books I collected myself, for I am an inveterate bibliophile.

When Mr Mole returned to the surgery that evening I handed him a copy of my list. I had written it out twice, and had put the original list into a filing cabinet because I strongly suspected that I might be able to use it again in my life as a country doctor.

'You might get a little inspiration from this!' I told him, handing him the product of my research.

(Editor's Note: A copy of the list the Doc gave to Mr Mole appears as an appendix at the back of this book.)

Mr Mole looked at the list with increasing astonishment. Then he looked up at me and smiled. 'OK,' he said. 'You win!' He looked at the list again and then shook his head. 'I'm astonished,' he admitted. 'This list is truly inspirational.' He looked at the list again. 'Painting was at the top of my list,' he said. 'I'd thought for some time that I'd like to try oil painting. But to be honest I thought I was too old.' He looked at my list again. 'Now I'm not so sure,' he said, with a beaming smile. 'I think I'll get myself to the nearest art shop, buy some canvas and some paints and see what I can do.'

He stood up, shook my hand and thanked me.

I felt pleased that my work in my library was appreciated.

As soon as the evening surgery was over I sat down to dinner. Patsy had thoughtfully prepared one of my favourite, simple meals: two fried eggs, a huge pile of chips and a good supply of onion rings. It wasn't a healthy meal but occasionally, when I've had a hard day I need what Patsy calls 'little boy food'. And this was definitely one of those days.

As I sat down to dinner I felt drained.

It had been a long, difficult day with rather too much drama for me. Patsy and I had already decided to watch an old black and white movie after dinner; possibly something starring Humphrey Bogart. Maybe *Casablanca* or *The Maltese Falcon*. We have a good collection of old black and white films on video tape. I prefer to watch films on video because if the telephone goes and I have to deal with a patient then I can stop the film for a while and carry on viewing afterwards. I have, over the years, missed the ends of more films than I care to remember through trying to watch them on the television.

We had put the children to bed and were sitting down to watch the film when the doorbell went. I stood up and with a weary body and a weary heart I made my way to the door.

It was 'Icy' Rhodes, the man whose knife wound I had sewn up earlier in the day.

'Just wanted to say thank you for sewing me up, doc,' he said. And he produced from behind his back a dead pheasant.

'Picked this up while I was out in the woods yesterday,' he said, handing me the bird.

I looked at the bird and then at him.

'Just a small 'thank you',' he explained. 'Very grateful to you.'

I took the bird which he was still holding out to me. I started to tell him that Patsy and I are vegetarian but the words wouldn't come out. The pheasant had a patch of grey hair on one side of its head and it had a bad foot. One of its tail feathers was missing.

I was about to hand the bird back to him but something in me stopped me doing so.

'See you in a couple of day then, doc,' said 'Icy'. He turned away and was swallowed up in the blackness of the night.

I shut the front door and took the pheasant into the house.

Patsy came into the hallway to see what was happening. She stared at me and then at the pheasant I was holding.

'Is that Percy?' she asked.

I was so upset I couldn't speak. I just nodded. Tears started to roll down my cheeks.

'What are you going to do with him?' she asked.

'I'm going to bury him,' I told her, in a whisper.

I took Percy outside with me and found a spade.

Patsy held the torch while I dug a hole and buried our friend. Tears rolled down our cheeks. We said a prayer for him. There would now be no fourth generation of pheasants having breakfast with us.

It had not been a day I wanted to repeat any time soon.

Frank's Astonishing Recovery

The consequences of a stroke can, of course, be devastating; both to the patient and to those who are close to him or her. Movement can be lost, mental skills may deteriorate or disappear and the patient may, to those around, appear to have lost all the skills which he or she had taken a lifetime to acquire.

But all those skills are not necessarily lost for ever.

They may be hidden; temporarily lost and temporarily unavailable.

And although the damage done by a stroke may, it is true, sometimes be permanent it is also often possible for the patient to recover lost abilities. The patient who has lost the ability to walk or to hold a pen or throw a ball may recover all those lost skills. The patient who has lost the power of speech, and who appears to have lost the ability to converse may, in time, make a startling recovery and recover most if not all of their lost abilities.

It used to be thought that a patient who had a stroke would stop recovering a few days or weeks after the stroke had occurred. It was believed that if the effects of a stroke were not overcome within a few months then there would be little or no chance of there being any future improvement.

But all this was wrong.

A patient who has had a stroke may continue to improve not for days, weeks or months but for years afterwards.

However, this improvement does not usually come easily. The patient will need a massive amount of help and support and encouragement if they are to have a chance of regaining those skills which have been lost.

In the immediate aftermath of a stroke, most patients who are aware of what has happened to them are, not surprisingly, depressed.

It must be terrifying to find, quite suddenly, that those basic abilities which you had taken for granted, are suddenly lost to you. It must be terrifying to find yourself unable to stand, walk, converse, read the paper or even clean your own teeth. It must be terrifying for someone who was formerly strong and independent to find themselves weak and dependent; quite unable even to feed themselves without assistance and, perhaps most frightening of all, incapable of making themselves understood.

Patients who have had a stroke face frustration, boredom, despair, depression and fear and those who are close to them suffer exactly the same horrifying mixture of emotions.

It was fortunate for us all that we realised that Frank could understand what we were saying. Right from the start we were able to institute a simple method of communication which enabled us to ensure not only that he understood what we were saying to him but that he, in turn, could communicate some of his thoughts and feelings to us.

By understanding that Frank could still understand us we avoided the awful possibility (so regrettably common among stroke victims) of the patient being treated as a child or an idiot by well-meaning relatives and friends.

Everyone around him understood that Frank had not lost all his abilities, and had not suddenly gone from being Frank to being a helpless child, but that he had simply lost the ability to use his body and his mind in the normal way.

Frank had suffered an illness and he needed our help.

In the days which followed, Frank's admission to what we think of as the Bilbury Cottage Hospital (but what the authorities prefer to think of as the Brownlow Country Hotel), it slowly became abundantly clear that I had made the right decision in not sending him to one of the major local hospitals.

No one except Patsy knew just how relieved I was when Frank's blood pressure came down and his condition did not worsen. It had probably been the most difficult decision I'd ever had to make as a doctor. I have made many mistakes in my life. I thanked God, Hippocrates, Aesculapius and St Damian that wasn't one of them.

And although we could not prove this, because no hospital tests were ever done, I was, I think, correct in assuming that Frank had suffered an intra-cerebral bleed caused by his high blood pressure.

I believe that if I had sent him to a hospital in Barnstaple or Exeter, Frank's condition could well have deteriorated. He would, I believe, have been more anxious and more frightened and there is a good chance that his blood pressure would have gone even higher.

No one can know any of this for sure, of course.

But what is clear is that Frank's blood pressure did come under control relatively speedily. And once his condition stabilised we were able to start thinking about his rehabilitation.

Bradshaw and I both checked Frank's muscle power, nerve capacities and so on twice a day and no doctor in the world has ever been more relieved when the tests which we did showed that our patient's condition was not deteriorating. The fact that it was not deteriorating meant that the bleed which had, I believe, caused the problem was not still causing damage.

There was no guarantee that Frank would not have another stroke, of course, but I was confident that if I could keep Frank's blood pressure as low as possible (partly with the right balance of prescription drugs, partly by filling him with confidence, partly by improving his general health and eradicating some of the bad habits which had put his body in peril in the first place and partly by ensuring that he remained calm and free of all unnecessary stresses) then we could start the long, slow process to recovery.

'Will he ever be able to walk again?' asked Gilly, three days after Frank had suffered his stroke. 'Will he be able to talk?'

Gilly's father had suffered a stroke and he had remained bedridden until his death just a few months later. Gilly's fears for Frank were, inevitably, coloured by her experience with her father. 'I believe that he will be able to walk and talk and help you run the Duck and Puddle,' I assured her, with a confidence which may not have been entirely genuine but which was, I believed, vital in giving her and Frank the faith that was necessary for his recovery. 'We'll work with him and we'll cajole and assist and, if necessary, bully him into doing everything that will help him make as full a recovery as possible. It will be hard and it may be slow and he may not make a complete recovery but we will get Frank back to being Frank.'

I'm still not sure just how much of this I really believed, of course.

Helping a stroke victim to recover lost skills can be, and usually is, a long and painful process. I did not know for certain that Frank would recover. But I did know for certain that I needed to instil confidence and belief in both Frank and Gilly.

If they did not truly believe that he would get better then the healing process would be infinitely more challenging and, quite possibly, utterly impossible.

The patient who accepts his plight as merely a consequence of fate, an unalterable punishment for past sins of omission or commission, will probably never make any meaningful recovery.

The relatives and friends who accept that the patient will never talk again or will never again be able to walk will probably find their fears to be self-fulfilling.

Of course, many stroke victims do not ever recover. Many suffer additional strokes. Some deteriorate, for a whole host of reasons, and fail to make any meaningful recovery.

But there are, no doubt, many who fail to make any recovery because they do not believe that recovery of any kind is ever really possible.

Right from the start, Frank had a number of things in his favour.

First and foremost he had a wife who loved him, who cared for him and who was prepared to fight tooth and nail for him.

Second, he was still living in the village where he felt comfortable and he was, therefore, surrounded by friends who also cared for him and who would, when asked, do everything in their power to help him make a good recovery.

Third, he was the only real patient in our hospital. The other two patients quickly recognised that Frank's need was far greater than their own and within hours they switched from being patients to being live-in members of staff. Over the weeks which followed Frank's admission, they remained in the hospital and they worked hard and with genuine enthusiasm to help speed his recovery. I'm not sure that either of them realised it but, of course, by dedicating themselves to Frank's recovery they put their own problems to one side and, I have no doubt, helped themselves recover and grow stronger. Their lives acquired real purpose and, as my conversation with Mr Mole had reminded me, few things give us more strength than having a target, an aim and a reason for living: a goal and a motive for each day.

Two days after Frank had been admitted to our small Bilbury hospital, I tried to arrange for a physiotherapist and a speech therapist to come over to help expedite his recovery. I might as well have tried to arrange for Frank to take a trip on the next rocket to the moon. It would have probably been easier.

Living in a small, isolated village like Bilbury has many advantages but it does mean that when it comes to obtaining outside help you are sometimes pretty near to the bottom of the queue. In a way, of course, it is understandable. Just travelling out to Bilbury and back again takes a good deal of time. And when a physiotherapist or speech therapist is travelling they won't be doing what they are paid to do. Still, it was a disappointment.

So, as is often the case in Bilbury, we were on our own. And it seemed to me to be clear that we had to prepare our own recovery programme to help Frank regain his lost skills. I knew from my own hospital experience that stroke patients who are left to their own devices make very little progress and, indeed, often tend to deteriorate. The patient who stays in bed and does nothing will lose increasing amounts of muscle power and before long, the limbs which were not affected by the stroke will also begin to lose function. And without stimulation the brain deteriorates still further too and an inability to communicate will be compounded by increasing frustration and boredom.

I had to recruit aides, assistants, therapists and teachers from among the Bilbury villagers. And I knew that I had to explain to every single one of them that Frank had not suddenly lost all his skills. Too many people (including professionals who really ought to know better) talk to stroke patients as if they were slightly backward children. This can be enormously depressing and painful for the patient whose brain is still functioning perfectly well but who has lost basic communication skills. I cannot begin to imagine how frustrating it must be for a man or woman to suddenly find themselves being patronised, talked down to and talked about when they can understand everything that is being said to them and about them but simply cannot respond with words or actions because their body will no longer respond in an appropriate manner.

All those who were going to help Frank had to understand that his lifetime of knowledge was still there, hidden inside his brain, and now simply had to be unlocked so that it could once again be accessed.

We needed to recruit as many people as possible who were prepared to give one or two hours a week to help Frank regain the physical and mental skills which he had lost. And we needed to start the programme as soon as we could; before Frank had time to become too upset and depressed by his condition.

My first decision was to plan a simple exercise programme. This had to be designed to help Frank regain the ability to use the side of his body that the stroke had paralysed. We needed to exercise the muscles, push them into working again and so enable him to use the leg and the arm that were lying useless; a hindrance rather than a help.

Without a professional physiotherapist to show us the ropes Bradshaw and I created a very simple regimen of exercises, and to make sure that Frank did not get too tired we decided to limit the physical part of his recovery to one hour every morning and one hour every afternoon. This would, we knew, be far more assistance than a patient in an ordinary hospital could possibly hope to receive.

We decided to fill as much of the rest of each day as we could with a programme of mental exercises designed to help Frank regain the use of his mind.

Since we didn't have any professionals to call on, this obviously meant that we had to compile a team of volunteers.

Gilly was obviously top of the list but she still had to run the Duck and Puddle. There was no question of closing the pub, for if the Duck and Puddle shut its doors, Frank and Gilly would have absolutely no income. They would, however, still have substantial outgoings. Since they were both officially classified as self-employed, they would not be able to claim any unemployment benefits.

Fortunately, Adrienne, my sister-in-law, came to Gilly's rescue by offering to help out behind the bar and in the kitchen. 'I hate hospitals of any kind and I'm absolutely no good at all with sick people,' Adrienne told Gilly with her usual disarming candour, 'but I desperately want to help somehow. So I'll help out at the Duck and Puddle for as many hours a day as you need me.'

And she was as good as her word.

Throughout the darkest months of Frank's recovery, she worked several hours a day at the Duck and Puddle and steadfastly refused to accept any payment. Gilly, it has to be said, responded by refusing to accept money from Patchy when he ate or drank at the pub.

Finding helpers who could help Frank perform simple muscle strengthening exercises, and then stand alongside him as he re-learnt how to walk, was not difficult. Everyone in the village liked Frank. He drank too much, smoked too much, ate too much, swore too much and had absolutely no time for bureaucrats, but these were vices with which people could sympathise. Whenever there was a storm, Frank would be the first man in the village to submit his insurance claim (and the first to help enhance the damage that had been done if it meant a bigger claim could be made) but few villagers could hold that against him since most of them did much the same sort of thing themselves. But if anyone in the village was going through a bad time Frank would always be among the first to help. He would give money he couldn't afford to give, pay a grocery bill at Peter Marshall's shop if he knew of some old villager who was having a hard time and give drinks 'on the slate' when he knew damned well that the customer would never be able to pay his bill and that the 'slate' would never be wiped clean.

And so, finding helpers who would volunteer to give a couple of hours a week to help Frank walk again was not difficult.

Within a fortnight Frank was out of bed, wandering slowly up and down the corridors of Dr Brownlow's sprawling old home. Within little more than a month he was wandering around the garden, always accompanied by two helpers (Frank is a big man and right from the start I made it a rule that whenever he was out of bed he would be assisted not by one but by two volunteers) and although progress might have appeared slow, it was steady and there wasn't a week that went by without someone saying that they couldn't believe just how much Frank had improved.

Putting together a rota of people prepared to help Frank regain his mental skills was always going to be more difficult. For one thing most people were rather frightened by the prospect of helping someone learn to speak again. And they were even more frightened, if that were possible, about the prospect of teaching someone how to recapture the parts of their mind which they had lost. Most people in the village had absolutely no experience, or knowledge, of what is, after all, a fairly specialised area of medicine.

But, to my astonishment and delight, we soon found that we had enough villagers to keep Frank occupied for three or even four hours a day. Patsy found herself in charge of preparing the rota of helpers and she fitted in those who were helping Frank relearn how to walk and use his arms with those who were helping him learn how to speak and think.

At first, we made the mistake of trying to capture Frank's imagination with books and magazines. Several volunteers tried encouraging him to relearn the alphabet or how to do simple crossword puzzles. This, however, was a mistake because Frank quickly became bored.

And then Thumper had a brainwave.

'Frank is never going to be interested in whether or not the cat sat on the damned mat,' he exclaimed, after finding one well-meaning old lady using a child's reading book to help Frank recover his literacy skills. 'Frank likes darts and dominoes and cards.'

And so we revised our teaching methods to incorporate games and skills which we knew Frank would find invigorating. And the teachers found these things far more exciting, too.

Thumper set up a dartboard and organised games of darts. To begin with, Frank's ability to throw darts was so poor that the wall surrounding the dartboard quickly became peppered with so many holes that it looked as if it had contracted woodworm. But the most important part of the game was undoubtedly the counting. Thumper made Frank keep score and waited, with surprising patience, while Frank worked out which section of the board the next player needed to aim at. Frank had never been a good darts player (he always used to say that he didn't like any sporting activity which required him to put down the glass he was holding and that darts was all right only if your glass was nearly empty and you weren't likely to spill any) but within a few weeks there was no one in the village who could beat him. Frank, who wasn't as slow as many believed, realised that the modestly skilful player who aims for the number 19 on the dartboard will almost always do better than the greedier player who aims for the 20. 'The thing is,' he told me confidentially one day, 'that if you aim at the 20 and miss then you'll probably score a 1 or a 5, but if you aim at the 19 and miss you'll hit the 3 or the 7. That's enough to give you an edge.'

Several of the spinster ladies who were helping were aghast when they came into the hospital and found Frank, Thumper, Patchy and me playing poker. But Frank loved those games and his recovery was, I believe, far faster because he was engaged than it would have been if we had tried to persuade him to do some basket weaving or draw pictures with crayons. Because Frank's concentration was poor, we would switch games several times an hour – moving from poker to whist to dominoes and back again.

And to help Frank's language skills Patchy found a wonderful, tattered, book which contained scores of recipes for old-fashioned cocktails. Frank loved that book and read it so much that he knew every word by heart. He had never been much of a man for cocktails (beer, gin and whisky had been his accustomed tipples) but now they became an important part of his life and a massive part of his recovery. When Patsy mentioned this in a letter she sent to the Rathbones, who were back in America, they sent over several American books about cocktail making. Frank loved these books and devoured the contents of these with the same unlimited enthusiasm. In return, Patsy and I regularly sent the Rathbones photographs of their ever-expanding porcine prize.

All these things gave Frank confidence and belief.

I kept him in the hospital for three months; not because he needed to stay there for so long but because I thought it would be easier for the volunteers to work with him in the spacious rooms of Dr Brownlow's old home than it would be to work with him in the Duck and Puddle. But when he went back to live at the Duck and Puddle, the volunteers all went with him, and Frank's daily recovery continued apace.

After six months, Frank was damned near back to where he had been before the stroke. He was a lot fitter too. He had lost two stones in weight and completely stopped smoking. I allowed him one or two small alcoholic drinks a day because I felt that he needed the reward and I knew that giving up everything at once would have been, perhaps, just too difficult. Even his diet changed. Gilly refused to make chips for him and he even began to enjoy the healthy meals she started to cook. Oddly enough, she told me that many of the other villagers who regularly ate at the Duck and Puddle chose to eat healthier food as they realised just how devastating the consequences of a poor diet could be. Pete Marshall, at the village shop, told me that he was selling just two thirds as many cigarettes and cigars as he had been selling before Frank was taken poorly that fateful night at the Duck and Puddle.

Frank's recovery gave the village a wonderful feeling of communal warmth. This was partly because just about everyone who lived in Bilbury had helped in one way or another. It was partly because it was wonderful to see someone overcome the terrible consequences of a stroke. But it was, I think, also because everyone was cheered to see that Frank had, with the help of his friends, proved that it is possible to recover from a stroke. Knowing that diminished the fear of a terrible illness. It meant that others might do the same.

The Surprise Pregnancy

'I know you'll probably think it pretty unlikely, but I think I'm pregnant, doctor.'

The new patient sighed, slumped down on the chair in front of me and looked at me as though daring me not to laugh.

I never laugh at patients, however outlandish or unexpected their condition might be.

'What makes you think you're pregnant?'

I've been putting on weight, I have difficulty in sleeping, my tummy is very swollen and every morning I feel nauseous.'

'Have you been sick?'

'I'm usually sick once or twice before breakfast. But then the sickness feeling gradually goes away.'

'Anything else?'

'I get backache quite a lot. I've never had any back trouble before. But for the last few weeks I've had a lot of back pain.'

I nodded and made some notes on the patient's folder.

'And I get cravings.'

'Cravings?'

'I ate two bags of pork scratchings the other evening. And I usually hate pork scratchings.'

I nodded and murmured something. 'How long has this been going on?' I asked.

'Three or four months now.'

'Have you ever had anything like it before?'

'No. Definitely not.'

I wasn't quite sure what question to ask next or if, indeed, there were any other appropriate questions to ask. So it seemed to me that the best action would probably to perform an examination.

'Pop behind the screen and slip your things off, and then climb up on the couch,' I said. 'I need to have a look at you.'

'How much do you need me to take off?'

'Everything down to your underwear,' I said.

Two minutes later Mr Porchester was lying on the couch, wearing only his underpants and socks, and I was examining his clearly swollen abdomen, desperately trying to decide what to do and say next. Since there were no breasts to be swollen and tender, and no vagina to be examined, my options were strictly limited.

'My breasts are sore too,' he said. He reached up and touched his left nipple. 'My nipples especially.'

Gently, I examined his chest. I wasn't entirely sure that I wasn't imagining it but I thought there was some swelling in the breast area.

'Am I going to have a baby?' he asked.

'No,' I said. 'I don't think that's very likely.'

'Oh,' he said. He sounded disappointed.

'It really isn't possible,' I pointed out. 'Your basic architecture isn't suited to either conception or to childbirth.'

He looked at me, thought for a moment, and then nodded. 'I suppose not,' he said. He seemed genuinely disappointed. I thought then, and still think, that although he knew that it was impossible for him to be pregnant, a small part of him rather hoped that he might be about to experience a real pregnancy and to give birth to the world's first such miracle baby. It occurred to me that the newspaper serial rights, the book rights and the film rights would be worth a fortune. Mr Porchester would become a millionaire overnight.

I took his pulse, checked his blood pressure and then weighed him. When I'd done all this, a sort of unusual pre-natal check I suppose, I told him that he could get dressed.

He put on his shirt and a pair of khaki shorts which he wears whatever the weather. I have seen him wearing shorts when there was snow on the ground. Whenever I see Mr Porchester I cannot help thinking that if God had intended men to wear shorts he would not have given them such knobbly knees.

'There really isn't anything I can give you,' I told him, when he was dressed and sitting down in front of me. 'Your symptoms will almost certainly disappear when your wife has had her baby.' Mr Porchester's unusual disorder was not unique. It is a registered medical disorder known as Couvade Syndrome. I asked him how his wife was doing, though I suspected that she was probably doing very well indeed. She usually does.

Potelmy told me that his wife was doing very well.

'I don't think she is ever healthier than she is when she's pregnant,' said Potelmy. 'That's the funny thing, really. She sails through her pregnancies without any discomforting symptoms.' He paused, thought for a moment, and then half smiled. 'And yet I'm now having all the symptoms that you might expect her to have.'

Mrs Porchester has a vast number of children and produces babies as effortlessly as a cat produces kittens. She once told me that she gets pregnant if a man comes within ten yards of her and she seems to be so fertile that for all I know she could well be telling the truth.

Potelmy Porchester is her fourth husband, though to be honest I seem to remember that she wasn't actually married to any of the first three, but that they were what is usually known as 'common law husbands'.

Potelmy owns to being the father of the three most recent children, though the fourth youngest does bear a remarkable resemblance to him and I have long suspected that the pair may have started their procreative activities some time before the relationship was formalised.

I have difficulty remembering how many children they have, let alone what all the children are called, but I haven't felt bad about this since I discovered that Mr and Mrs Porchester both have the same problem. They are the only married couple I know who have photographs of all their children pinned up on a board in their kitchen. Alongside each photograph is the child's name and the date of his or her birth. They introduced this sensible system when one of the boys celebrated his twelfth birthday without so much as a card, let alone a present. The poor boy went through the whole day expecting his parents and siblings to yell 'surprise' and to overwhelm him with cards, gifts and a cake. He only realised that his birthday had been completely forgotten when his Mum tucked him up in bed and gave him a goodnight kiss. The hapless parents realised that they had erred when one of the other boys reported that the birthday boy was sobbing his heart out. Potelmy hurried round to Peter Marshall's emporium and purchased the requisite articles, bringing them home just in time to celebrate the birthday. They had just ninety minutes to spare.

I told Potelmy to come back to see me in a couple of weeks for another pre-natal check-up. I even gave him one of the little cards I usually hand out to mothers-to-be and which includes advice on diet, weight, exercise, sexual activity and so on. There really wasn't much point in it, of course, but the medical profession knows very little about Couvade syndrome and I thought it might be a good idea to keep an eye on his blood pressure. I also thought it might help him cope more readily if he thought that someone was taking his condition seriously. I made a note to telephone the medical library at the British Medical Association building in London and to ask them to send me any recent medical papers they could find relating to the disorder. Not for the first time I found myself looking forward to the time when it will, I am sure, be possible to consult medical libraries from afar by using a computer.

To be honest, I wasn't all that surprised at Potelmy's seemingly bizarre condition. When I was a student at medical school, I saw a man with a similar pseudo pregnancy condition and the memory of that patient has, not surprisingly perhaps, stayed with me.

Men suffering from Couvade Syndrome invariably experience some or all of the symptoms their wife or girlfriend shows. Just what causes the misconception is a real mystery.

The term was first used in the 1860s to refer to rituals that have, over the centuries, been recorded in various societies. For example, in Ancient Egypt, a new father would take to his bed when his wife gave birth. And among the Cantabri people there was a custom whereby a new father-to-be would complain of labour pains and go to bed immediately his wife started to deliver her baby. He would then be treated as though he were pregnant. Similar rituals were not uncommon among other cultures – including in China and Russia and parts of the American continent. The idea, it is thought, may have been a conscious or unconscious effort to ward off evil demons and spirits by distracting them and, thereby, protecting the new mother and her vulnerable new born baby.

Some doctors believe that Couvade is an entirely psychosomatic disorder. In France, in the 1920s, it was believed that the syndrome usually occurred in marriages where the female partner was the dominant one. Others now wonder if there could possibly be a hormonal influence – with the wife's hormones having an influence on her husband's body. This sounds strange but it is known that similar things do happen. For example, if two women live or work closely together then it is quite common for them to find that their menstrual periods begin to coincide – even though they may have been some days apart at the start of the relationship. I wonder if, in the future, researchers might find that men experience changes in testosterone, oestradiol and prolactin levels when their spouse becomes pregnant.

Most men who develop symptoms of pregnancy have wives who are pregnant. It's almost as though the condition, and the associated symptoms, are catching.

Potelmy's wife, Lemuela, is seven months pregnant with her umpteenth child though, as Potelmy said, she has not really shown any of the usual signs of pregnancy. Her abdomen is swollen, of course, and she is obviously pregnant. But she has had none of the uncomfortable or unpleasant symptoms sometimes associated with pregnancy. Lemuela is perfect proof of the fact that although there may occasionally be problems, pregnancy is definitely not an illness – and a healthy pregnancy should never be treated as an illness unless there are signs or symptoms which need to be treated.

Lemuela has shelled out all her babies with consummate ease and I am confident that the latest birth will be just as free of complications. She reminds me of a newspaper editor I once knew in London. She took the morning off when she had her first baby but was back in her office the same afternoon. Unbelievably, she had a breakfast meeting with two American agents before she went to the delivery room. Lumuela doesn't have a job outside the home but if she did have then I am pretty certain that she too would be back at work within hours. Personally, I don't think it's a good idea. I'm old-fashioned enough to believe that the human body needs a little time to rest and recover after a traumatic event such as childbirth. But I suspect that I am a little out-of-date in my thinking as far as this is concerned. And I guess I'm going to be really out-of-date by the time the 1980s arrive in a few years' time.

After Mr Porchester had left, I found myself wondering how Potelmy would cope when it came time for Lemuela to have her baby.

The Porchester Confinements

In the good old, bad old days, before the discovery of penicillin and other such pharmacological goodies, all general practitioners were on call more or less permanently, and they had to learn to live with the sometimes untimely and always haphazard calls for attention that come a family doctor's way.

But things have changed, and now that we have somehow found ourselves living in the high tech world of the 1970s, most general practitioners work in groups and share their responsibilities for on call duties at night, at weekends or over bank holidays.

This sharing of on call responsibilities has changed life for those doctors working in cities, towns and larger villages.

Doctors who would, a generation ago, have been accustomed to being forever on duty can now sit down in front of their television set in an evening confident that they will be able to watch the beginning and the end of the same programme; they can sit down to meals knowing that they can take their time and enjoy their food without being constantly aware that if the telephone rings they will probably be eating cold food.

But here in Bilbury nothing much has changed, and I still practise medicine as it was practised half a century ago. (Although I do, of course, have the wonder of penicillin to call upon.)

I am on call 24 hours a day, seven days a week and 365 days a year because I work alone and the nearest doctors are too far away for us to arrange to share our night time or weekend responsibilities.

Today, it is, of course, the telephone that can make life particularly exhausting. It's like an electronic cuckoo: always screaming for attention and apparently never satisfied.

Like most doctors who practise alone, I have a special telephone which is designed to ring whenever some other piece of essential household equipment is activated. Our telephone will, for example, always ring if I lie down in the bath, turn on the television to watch a

74

programme to which I have been looking forward or try to boil a kettle.

If Patsy puts a hot meal down on the table then the telephone will immediately start to ring. How it knows to do that I really have no idea; but it does.

To ensure that I cope with the stress of the telephone well enough to live long enough to see next year's daffodils, I have devised a number of ways to relax.

I am, for example, an enthusiastic gardener, and although I don't much like the fiddly tasks such as weeding I very much enjoy taking dead branches off trees and chopping them up into fireplace sized logs. I also enjoy breaking up the smaller branches into kindling. You can't start a start a fire without a good supply of kindling and a few crumpled up pages of newspaper or a handful of junk mail. We can always find an old newspaper or a pile of unsolicited mail lying around but we have to collect our kindling. And there are few apparently dull tasks which I find more rewarding than collecting a bag full of nice, dry kindling.

And, of course, at the end of a session in the garden there is the bonus of being able to have a bonfire to get rid of all the bits of brushwood.

Sometimes I put the stuff I am burning into the incinerator (my new toy) and sometimes, if there is too much to fit in the incinerator, I just build a huge bonfire.

Patsy often says that if I wasn't a doctor I would probably be a professional pyromaniac. I just respond by telling her that it is perfectly possible to be both at the same time.

One late summer day I was planning a really good bonfire with my friend William, a GP who works in a large practice in the English midlands. He was staying with us for a few days; accompanied as usual by his wife and two children.

William's wife, Brenda, together with Patsy and our two small children, were in the house. The two women were baking cakes for a forthcoming village fete being held to raise money for the Bilbury Cottage Hospital. (For administrative reasons the Bilbury Cottage Hospital is, of course, known as the Brownlow County Hotel. This nomenclature is designed to confuse National Health Service bureaucrats but it confuses me too.) Our two little ones were 'helping'. They are specialists in both the 'tasting' and the 'making a mess' departments.

William and I, and William's two children, one of whom is aged six and the other is aged eight, were in our front garden. We were all busy collecting twigs and small branches which had come down from our big willow tree.

As we collected together the kindling, a middle-aged woman jogged very slowly past. I think most people in decent health would have been able to overtake her if they'd been going at a fairly ordinary walking pace. The woman, a patient of mine, waved and wheezed something indistinct which was probably 'Hello, doctor!'

'Ruddy joggers,' muttered William as she went past. 'It seems to be the health fad of the 1970s.'

'I wish she'd give up the jogging,' I muttered back. 'She's already got a bad back and one bad hip. If she doesn't give up jogging she'll soon have another bad hip and two bad knees to add to her collection.'

'I've had endless problems with patients jogging to get fit and lose weight,' said William. 'A good many of them make themselves ill.' He paused to break a decent length of willow into several smaller pieces and then tossed the twigs into the wheelbarrow. 'I'm utterly convinced that most joggers do themselves far more harm than good.'

'Oh, surely some of them do themselves a bit of good,' I protested.

'No,' said William, emphatically. 'No damned good at all! I had a female patient who was at least six stones overweight. She had a bum as big as Yorkshire. She knew she needed to lose weight but instead of eating less she decided to exercise more. An utterly daft idea, of course, because it was never going to work. She would exercise for 30 minutes and use up 200 calories, if that, and then she'd treat herself to a packet of biscuits and a large Coca Cola. Every time she exercised, she ended up eating more calories than she'd used up and so she steadily put on more and more weight. Eventually, she damaged a knee with her damned jogging and had to go into hospital for an operation. While she was there she contracted one of those nasty hospital infections. She was dead in less than a week. Nice woman, too. She left a lovely husband and three decent kids. What an absolute tragedy. If she hadn't taken up jogging she'd still be alive.'

We were both musing on this tragic irony when I heard a shout, looked up and saw Patsy standing at the front door. Her hands and forearms were covered with flour and she was holding the noisy end of the telephone high in the air – the long established sign telling me that there was a call for me.

The call was from Ptolemy Porchester, who was ringing to tell me that his wife, Lemuela was about to give birth to their latest child.

I exchanged my wellington boots for a pair of shoes, brushed some of the leaves and twigs off my jumper (my philosophy is, I'm afraid, that if you live in the country and you telephone the doctor out of hours then you must put up with him arriving in whatever he was wearing when you called – unless he was in bed or in the bath, of course) and clambered into the car, wondering to myself why Mrs Porchester, who seems to collect babies in the same sort of indiscriminate way that some people collect stamps or china elephants, prefers the Government's free milk and cod liver oil to its free contraceptives.

The baby had been well and truly born by the time I got there. The placenta and umbilical cord were sitting, neatly laid out, on a plate on the dressing table.

After having so many children, both Mrs Porchester and her latest baby always seem perfectly capable of dealing with that part of the exercise without any help from me. All I had to do was a little light needlework to tidy up the new mother's business end.

I think that Mrs Porchester must be taking part in some sort of competition to see who in Devon can have the most babies, and her primary thought after having one baby is always about doing the spade work for the conception of the next. And with this in mind Mrs Porchester always insists on having 'things down below tidied up and tightened a little'.

As I washed my hands in the bathroom next door, I listened to Mrs Porchester tell me, for the umpteenth time, how my predecessor Dr Brownlow, had once sewn his surgical glove into her interior back in the days when she had so few children that she knew all their names.

Mrs Porchester has a loud voice (not surprising, I suppose, when you have as many children as she has) but I was spared the repeat of the anecdote by the fact that Mr Porchester was sitting downstairs watching a football match on their old ten inch screen black and white television set. To compensate for his deafness, and the noise the children were making (they were playing pirates up and down the stairs), he had the sound turned up so high that when I began stitching, the silk thread I was using started to vibrate whenever I pulled it tight.

I made a mental note to tell Mr Porchester to visit the surgery to have his ears syringed. I have never known anyone produce as much ear wax as Mr Porchester and the level of his deafness inevitably rises as the wax accumulates.

My predecessor, Dr Brownlow, hated television sets even more than he hated seeing women in trousers and men wearing clip on bow ties and he detested the memory of the unfortunate John Logie Baird with the quiet dedication that most doctors reserve for Alexander Graham Bell. The thing he hated most about television sets was the fact that patients sometimes left them switched on when he was visiting and trying to examine a patient. He once gave me a valuable piece of advice about television sets. He told me that he had discovered that if he walked over to the seat and fiddled with all the knobs and dials he could cause so much distress to the viewer that the lesson would be well remembered. 'I gather,' he said, 'that when you mess around with the dials controlling tone and picture quality you can cause a degree of electronic confusion which can take many hours to put right.' He was right, of course. Messing with the controls of a television set will leave the owners watching programmes through a snow storm. Years after Dr Brownlow had died, I visited houses where the television set was unplugged and covered with a cloth the moment I walked through the door. Mr Porchester was the solitary exception in the village.

By the time I had finished sewing up Mrs Porchester to her satisfaction (she always insists that I restore her to the sort of aperture she, and indeed her husband, might have enjoyed on her wedding night and when I have finished sewing she always checks my handiwork with a couple of fingers), the football match was over and the television sound had been turned down.

I tottered down the stairs, making my way cautiously between dead and dying pirates and abandoned wooden swords, to find that Mr Porchester had poured me a small glass of cooking sherry in celebration. He offered me a very small cigar, as he always does and, as I always do, I thanked him and refused the offer. The sherry is bad enough but it can at least be swallowed like a dose of unpleasant medicine. I hate to think what the cigars must taste like for they smell far worse than my bonfires. The youngest of the pirates who had survived the 'Battle of the Stairs' seemed to be endeavouring to find out how much noise you can make when you bang toy cars onto dolls' heads. The older survivors were attempting to persuade their father to give them a glass of sherry to share.

I was keen to get away from there as quickly as I could for once she has delivered her latest baby, it has become customary for Mrs Porchester to cook her placenta and serve it up with a few braised onions and fried tomatoes. She says it's a pity to waste such a valuable source of nutrients. I believe that she and Potelmy share it between them, accompanied with a nice bottle of homemade parsnip and elderberry wine. I lived in dread that they might one day invite me to join them at their kitchen table on an evening when they share this curious, almost cannibalistic, repast. Although I suppose it would be possible for me to refuse any such offer on the grounds that I am a vegetarian. 'How are you feeling?' I asked Potelmy, very conscious of the fact that he had been suffering from Couvarde syndrome or a sympathetic pregnancy.

'Oh, I'm much better,' he said. He pulled up his shirt and undid his trousers to show me that his swollen abdomen was now quite flat. 'All my symptoms disappeared when Apple was born.'

'Apple?' I said. I'd never heard of anyone naming a child after a fruit.

'That's what we're calling the newborn,' Potelmy told me. 'We're great Beatles fans. And we like fruit.'

It seemed an odd name to give a child but then, I suppose, it is no stranger to name a child after a fruit than it is to name one after a flower and there are plenty of girls called 'Daisy', 'Rose' and 'Primrose'. I secretly rather hoped, however, that parents didn't start naming their children after vegetables.

I was relieved that Mr Porchester's pregnancy had gone well and was now over. I had been worrying what I would say, or do, if he asked me to sew him up.

'Could you give me my postnatal check-up now,' he asked me.

I took his blood pressure and told him that all seemed well. I honestly couldn't think of anything else to do. I could, I suppose, have suggested doing an anal examination, the closest thing possible to a vaginal examination, but he seemed happy enough with my having taken his blood pressure.

'Don't forget to pop along to the surgery to have your ears syringed,' I told him.

When I got back to Bilbury Grange, William and his two children were still tearing up newspapers and screwing up the torn pages into twists suitable for fire lighting. They had run out of old newspapers and had been into the kitchen to fetch the edition which had arrived that morning and which I had not yet had a chance to look at.

'Why were you so long?' asked Peter, William's son, as we struggled to unscrew the papers which contained the latest, end of season cricket results. It was a week old newspaper but I tend to read old newspapers far more avidly than I read new ones.

'I had to sew up a patient who'd just had a baby,' I explained.

William's son knows as much as most people about these things and I suspect that he is a constant source of educational material for his fellow pupils at his preparatory school.

(There are rumours that in some parts of the country, children are taught about these things in specially prepared sex education classes. If they ever introduce such things in Bilbury then the new village schoolmistress, who has taken over from our gardener's wife, will doubtless have to be supplemented. I rather doubt if our new school ma'am is well informed on such matters. She is a spinster, of a certain age, and she recently asked me if I thought it was possible that one of the village girls who had 'got herself into trouble' could have got that way through, as she had apparently claimed, attending a mixed bathing party on the beach at Combe Martin.)

I looked around the garden and wondered what other trees might need pruning and where I could best plant some fast growing varieties of silver birch – a tree which produces an excellent supply of kindling – when I heard William's son asking his father a question.

'If you've sewn her up,' said Peter, 'does that mean that she's decided to stop having babies?' He paused and looked hard at me. 'Or will someone have to go round and take out the stitches if she wants another one?'

'Your Dad will be able to answer that one,' I said, with shameful cowardice. 'I must just go and check on something in the house.'

Our two children are far too young to ask questions of such a sophisticated nature. I will deal with the problem of how to answer such queries when the time comes.

I have no doubt that William had an answer to that question and I suppose I should have hung around to find out what it was.

But I tottered indoors, clutching the bits and pieces of the sports pages which I had managed to salvage, and put on the kettle.

Naturally, the telephone began to ring.

The life of a country doctor is many things but it is never dull. Tragedy and comedy are never more than a telephone call away.

The Auction at Doone Cottage

I was sitting in my study trying to work my way through some paperwork which had accumulated.

In my world (and I suspect it is not a world I inhabit alone) the paperwork always seems to accumulate faster than I can deal with it. On my desk there was a boxful of receipts which needed to be filed ready for the taxman's annual bureaucratic extravaganza, several letters from health service bureaucrats which needed attention and some bills which needed paying.

I doubt if I am alone in the world in not enjoying administration. I would rather trim hedges with hand shears than sit and plough through a pile of dull paperwork.

I was rescued from this tedious chore by the arrival of my good friend and brother-in-law Patchy Fogg, antique dealer and old-fashioned wheeler dealer, whose voice I heard loud and clear, even though he came in through the kitchen door and my study cum surgery is at the other side of the house.

Patchy does not shout, or at least I've never heard him shout, but he has a voice which carries and if he ever found work as a racecourse commentator, he would be able to do his job without the aid of either a microphone or a loudspeaker system.

'You busy?' asked Patchy, bursting into my room like a force of nature.

Patsy, who was standing behind him, shrugged her shoulders and pulled a face which said, better than words, 'I tried to stop him but you know Patchy, he never likes being told he can't do something'. She was baking thick cut Devon pasties, using potatoes, swedes, tomatoes and herbs from our garden, and had somehow managed to get flour onto her blouse and into her hair. She was holding her hands, which were white, away from her body but the caution was now pointless.

When I first moved to Bilbury I knew absolutely nothing about antiques. I could hardly tell walnut from mahogany and, whatever it was that I was looking at, I was quite incapable of differentiating between the genuine article and a copy made in Hong Kong circa 1961.

But over the years, Patchy has taught me quite a good deal.

I have learned to tell a davenport from a bureau from a Victorian writing slope and to tell when an auctioneer is taking bids from an imaginary bidder (known as taking bids 'off the wall') in order to boost the price of something he was selling at auction.

(According to Patchy, when auctioneers for the big, posh, London auctioneers do this it is called 'taking bids off the chandeliers'.)

I have learned that the oldest English furniture is usually made of oak for two very simple reasons. First, when it became feasible and fashionable to furnish castles and houses with tables and chairs and storage chests the commonest tree in England was the oak. Second, it is possible to carve oak timbers into the shapes required with the aid of an axe and an adze – the two tools commonly available.

We have an oak dole cupboard in Bilbury Grange which Patchy found for us. It originally stood outside a monastery wall and was regularly filled with bread so that poor travellers could help themselves. That was, incidentally, the original use of the word 'dole'.

As the years went by, so oak gradually went out of fashion. In the 17th century, Charles II preferred elegant walnut furniture because, being easier to carve, walnut could be made into more artistic shapes and covered with fancier additions. Oak is a hard wood which is difficult to shape with hand tools.

And then, in the 18th century, mahogany, imported from India, was the wood of choice and English furniture became even more complex and carefully designed.

Thanks to Patchy, I had learned to beware of shops which had signs across their windows screaming 'Lease Expiring' and 'Closing Down Sale', for these are, he told me, tricks which are well known in the antiques and jewellery trades. Patchy told me he knew of a shop in Birmingham which had been attracting innocent customers with its 'Closing Down' signs for at least ten years. The customers all thought that they were getting bargain prices but they weren't, of course.

Patchy taught me to use my hands as well as my eyes when examining furniture. 'Genuinely old furniture has a softness to it, a warmth all of its own,' said Patchy, who had a reputation throughout Devon for being able to identify a genuine antique almost instantly.

'There's an auction at the other end of the village,' said Patchy, slumping down into the chair normally used by patients. 'It's at a place called Doone Cottage, somewhere along the road to North Ilkerton. I picked up the estate agent's particulars this morning and today's the viewing day. I thought I might go and have a look at what they've got for sale. But I really can't bear the idea of schlepping over there by myself. Can you bear to drag yourself away from all that exciting looking paperwork for an hour or two?'

I put down the sheaf of papers I was holding and grinned at him. 'I'd be your man if you'd invited me to a shoe shop opening,' I told him, 'I was just trying to understand a letter from the local health service administrator. It would have made more sense if it he'd written back to front in Latin.' The administrator had a habit of writing to all the local family doctors at least twice a week. Since he never used one word when ten would do just as well, his letters took some deciphering. I had got into the habit of going through his letters with a pen in my hand. I would then scratch out all the obviously superfluous words and phrases and then try to make sense of what was left.

As we drove off, I told Patchy that I knew exactly how to find Doone Cottage since the owner, Mrs Gladys Ptolemy, who had died recently, had been a patient of mine.

Patchy explained that the sale had been organised by Harley House an appropriately named local estate agent from Barnstaple, whose red and white House For Sale signs were a well-known sight in North Devon. The main item in the sale was a modest sized cottage with a small but decent garden but the entire contents of the house were also included with the cottage since Mrs Ptolemy the former owner, now deceased, had left her entire estate to a nephew whom she hadn't seen for years. He lived in Leeds in the North of England and hadn't even bothered to come down to Devon for the funeral.

Mrs Gladys Ptolemy, who always insisted on being addressed by her full name, had been a patient of mine and had recently succumbed, after a long illness, to kidney failure. She had been 96 when she'd died and in the old days, the family doctor would have probably simply written 'old age' on the death certificate. These days coroners insist on having rather more precise details put on their bit of paper and so she officially died of 'kidney failure', though to be honest I could have just as easily written 'heart failure' or 'liver failure'. The truth was that her body had, quite simply, run out of time on the celestial warranty.

Mrs Ptolemy was the only person I ever met who had been born on the island of Lundy, a very solid lump of granite which sticks up out of the sea off the North Devon coast. I sometimes thought that perhaps the peculiarity of her birth might perhaps have changed her outlook on life in some way. She often talked about the fact that she had been born on an island and clearly thought that in some way it made her 'special'. And I suppose it did: it was certainly true that she was one of the very few people in the world who was able to say that they had been born on an island which is just three miles long and no more than half a mile wide. The sad thing is, I suppose, that it was the only part of her life that she felt made her different; important even. I think I felt rather sorry for her that she could never remember the only truly memorable thing that ever happened in her life.

Lundy is a surprisingly fertile piece of rock. Patsy and I went there for a day trip when Dr Brownlow was still alive and it was easier for me to be away from the village. There is good fishing in the sea around Lundy and the soil on top of the island is surprisingly fertile, providing lush grass for the sheep who are by far the most numerous inhabitants. There are quite a few plants, including one horticultural speciality known as the Lundy Cabbage, which are found only on the island. Indeed, there is an insect called the Bronze Lundy Cabbage Flea Beetle which lives only on the Lundy Cabbage. Since the plant is exclusively indigenous to Lundy so is the Bronze Lundy Cabbage Flea Beetle.

I remembered from our visit that the island has a pub called the Marisco Tavern and a few grey houses, and there is a 13th century castle too. But although the castle was built with walls three feet thick the building is now just a ruin. The storms which have lashed the island for centuries have destroyed man's handiwork. The castle, so they say, was built by Henry III using money he made by selling the rabbits which were caught on the island. Back in those days Lundy was an official Royal warren and the rabbits were an important source of revenue for the monarch.

Visitors sometimes call the place Lundy Island but that's tautological because the word Lundy is Norse for 'Puffin Island', so to call it Lundy Island is like calling it 'Puffin Island Island'. Modern tourists visit Lundy to watch the birds, clamber about on the rocks or just to say they've been there. Many buy a Lundy stamp which isn't a proper postage stamp in that it can't be used to mail a letter, but it can be stuck on an envelope together with a stamp issued by the Royal Mail or stuck in a stamp album on one of those pages they always put at the back for 'oddities'.

The strange thing is that although Mrs Ptolemy was born on the island, her parents didn't live there. They were visiting on a day trip and Mrs Ptolemy was born a fortnight early, delivered by a midwife who, fortuitously, happened to be in the same party of tourists. Mrs Ptolemy and her parents had to stay the night in a local's cottage until mother and baby were well enough to make the return journey. I have often wondered what sort of people would make a potentially rough sea trip so close to the mother-to-be's due delivery date. When Patsy was expecting, I found myself worrying if she went too far down the garden. In the end, I persuaded her to carry an old bicycle horn so that she could 'toot' for help if she needed it.

I had been to Doone Cottage on numerous occasions and I couldn't remember ever seeing anything there that was likely to raise the blood pressure of an antique dealer. I had never spotted any expensive looking items of furniture or any majestic paintings just waiting to be 'discovered' and carted off to a London auction room.

I know that there are doctors, particularly those working in rural areas, who will examine the contents of an elderly patient's home with great care; drawing attention to those items which take their fancy in the hope that they will be given the item as a present, or at least left it in the patient's will. I know of one doctor, working not a million miles away from Bilbury, who frequently offers to buy furniture or pictures which he recognises as having value. He tells the patient that the chair, bookcase, dressing table or whatever would look good in his own home and that hc will pay the patient a good price for it. The price is never a 'good' one, of course, and the item soon ends up in an auction or an antique dealer's shop with the doctor's wallet a good deal heavier as a result. I could never do that. One elderly patient once insisted on giving me a book which he thought I would like. I did, indeed, like the book but it was a valuable first edition and I felt embarrassed and ashamed to take such a gift. When the patient wasn't looking I sneaked it back onto his shelves.

It isn't only doctors who do this sort of thing, of course.

Delivery men, workmen of all types, chimney sweeps and insurance agents have all been known to express interest in things they spot in people's homes. The owner of the home (and the antique) will usually be elderly, frail and probably short of money. Such individuals are easy prey for the skilful trickster. Tricking the elderly into parting with the treasures for less than they are worth seems to me to be a pretty low way to make a living. Patchy said he knew a chimney sweep who used to look out for pieces of furniture which had old worm holes in them. If there are three or four old pieces of furniture in a room there is a very good chance that at least one will show signs of woodworm. The worm holes will usually be old and of no consequence but whenever he spotted a piece of furniture with evidence of worm infestation the sweep would suck in his breath, shake his head and warn the house owner of the danger of having worm infested furniture in their home.

'It'll affect your other furniture and then the structure of your house,' he'd say, feigning sympathy.

He would then offer to take away the affected item to use for firewood.

But he wouldn't chop it up, of course.

Instead, he would take it straight to a dealer and sell it for a very good profit with no risk and no expenditure. If the holes were noticeable, the dealer would fill them in and varnish over them.

It is often said that one should never speak ill of the dead, and though I understand and sympathise with the feeling that one should not speak ill of people who are no longer around to defend themselves I don't think this means that one should never tell the truth about the dead.

And the truth about Mrs Gladys Ptolemy is, I'm afraid, that she was not a particularly pleasant or warm-hearted person.

She was one of those people, of whom there never seems to be a shortage in the world, who must always be the centre of attention.

Such folk are forever convinced that other people exist to do their bidding and that the even strangers are always waiting for their instructions, their advice and their judgements. She was completely confident that she knew all there was to know about medicine, finance, the law, the church and politics. And her understanding of human emotions was, in her mind, as unlimited as her willingness to share her understanding with others. Every day she wrote dozens of letters and notes. Some of these were posted in the ordinary way (if she ran out of stamps she did not allow this to hinder her, simply ordering someone to pop the letters in the post-box and allow the recipient to pay the postage) and some were handed out to be hand delivered. Kind-hearted locals who called in to do shopping or gardening for her were invariably sent off around the village delivering hand-written notes. She sent instructions and recommendations to everyone whom she felt might benefit from her wisdom. She sent notes to the vicar suggesting subjects for his sermons. She advised the local constable on the best way to deal with any offenders whom he encountered. She shared her views on town planning and highway maintenance with the appropriate authorities and she wrote to our local Member of Parliament on a weekly basis – giving him clear instructions on how he should vote on important issues of the day. To her neighbours she boldly suggested suitable romances and recommended separations and divorces and she campaigned tirelessly and aggressively for causes she espoused – causes which invariably were ones which affected her personally. I remember she took against a large ash tree which stood on someone else's land and which she felt impeded her view of a distant church which she rather liked. She wrote regularly to everyone she could think of, demanding that the tree be felled without delay. She said it was dangerous (which it wasn't), that it was dying (which it wasn't), that it was ugly (which it wasn't), that it interfered with her drains (which it didn't) and that other people wanted it removed (which they didn't).

As Mrs Ptolemy got older, and slightly frail, many people in the village tried to help her but she treated them all appallingly. Over the years at least four people had cut her lawn and tended her garden and none of them had ever charged her for their work but she had treated them all with such contempt that they had given up. Henry Templeton, having spent three hours working on her garden without so much as the offer of a glass of water, let alone a cup of tea, once asked if he could use her privy but was told that he could not and that he could damned well use a hedge instead. 'You bloody gypsies are all the same,' she shouted at him. Since Henry was a retired airline pilot, who had been cutting her grass and trimming her bushes out of the kindness of his heart, he thought this a little rich even for an eccentric old lady.

I once went round to her house at 4.00 a.m. and found myself ordered to trim her toenails which she had suddenly decided were too long. 'You look as if you got dressed in the dark!' she shouted at me, as I bent at her feet. She was quite right but given the time of night and the circumstances and the fact that she had told me on the telephone that she needed help urgently I did not feel that this was entirely reprehensible. I was, it is true, wearing a jumper which I had put on back to front and inside out but if she had been truly in need of urgent medical attention, as she had led me to believe, I cannot believe that she would have noticed or cared.

On another occasion I got there late at night and she shouted, 'Who are you?' when I knocked on the door. I told her it was me. I was standing on the doorstep and it was pouring with rain. There was no porch at all. No shelter from the rain.

'What do you want?' she demanded. 'If I'd wanted you to come round I'd have invited you.'

'You did invite me!' I shouted back. 'It's the doctor.'

Eventually she let me in.

It turned out that she had called for me because she thought she might have arthritis in her left knee. When I could find nothing wrong she told me I was a 'quack' and that she would call for a proper doctor next time she needed advice.

Every time I saw her she told me that she had a weak heart and that her mother and her grandmother, both of whom lived to be well into their nineties, had suffered with the same problem. Not until she was well into her nineties did I ever detect any problems with her heart. And she, like her mother and grandmother, lived to a fairly ripe old age.

It would have been easy to argue that her behaviour was a result of oncoming dementia but it would have been a dishonest and disingenuous argument. There was nothing wrong with Mrs Gladys Ptolemy other than the fact that she was a bad-tempered old woman.

She had been a rude and bad tempered woman in her middle years and, quite probably, a rude and bad tempered woman when she had been young.

Thumper once said that the village was divided about her. On the one hand there were those who believed that she was a kindly, sensitive and misunderstood old woman. On the other hand there were those who thought she was a bad tempered old bat. The first group consisted of Mrs Ptolemy herself and no one else. The second group, said Patchy, included everyone else in the locality.

My first thought, when we arrived at Doone Cottage, was that Patchy was probably wasting his time, since there didn't seem to be anything worth the attention of an antique dealer rather than a junk man. I, on the other hand, was happy to have found an excuse to leave behind the paperwork sitting on my desk.

I harboured a secret hope that it might, perhaps, sort itself out in my absence.

There were the usual vans parked on the verge, and three or four Volvo estate cars had been abandoned on the grass outside the cottage. All had the tell-tale heavy duty racks fitted to their roofs. I think it is probably safe to say that if you ever see an estate car with a strong looking luggage rack fitted then it will almost certainly be owned by an antique dealer.

When we arrived, Patchy said 'hello' to the agent, Harley House, a man he clearly knew well.

Harley is an imposing fellow, around six foot six inches tall and sufficiently well-built never to have to worry about being described as thin. He likes pies, not particularly caring about the filling they contain, and has eaten a good many of them in his life. If you put him on one side of a scale and a small family car on the other it would be impossible to say which side would go down and which would go up. I have sat with him in the Duck and Puddle and watched him eat three of Gilly's family sized steak and kidney pies at a single sitting.

Harley is completely bald and whatever the weather he always wears a hat. In the winter he wears a brown trilby and in the summer he favours a Panama. North Devon can be quite a windy part of the world, and Harley has on many occasions conducted out door auctions with one hand holding his lot sheet and the other holding his hat in position.

He once told me that he has worn a hat since he read that Aeschylus, the Greek writer who died in 456 BC at the age of 69, met his maker when a short-sighted eagle dropped a tortoise on his head. Apparently, according to Harley, the eagle mistook the bald playwright's head for a rock and dropped the tortoise in order to break it open and get at the meat inside.

I remember mentioning that there are, as far as I am aware, very few eagles left in North Devon, and probably even fewer free range tortoises, but Harley, who has many fine qualities but is not a man blessed with an overenthusiastic sense of humour, pointed out, quite sternly, that it is much better to be safe than sorry. He added, I recall, that, as a medical man, I should be aware that an ounce of prevention is worth far more than a good many bottles of medicine.

Inside Doone Cottage, the usual array of dealers and collectors had been joined by a few neighbours. I have little doubt that the neighbours were there, as is often the case, more out of simple nosiness than out of any genuine interest in making a purchase. It is true that one or two of them had probably tottered round in the hope that they might be able to purchase an item which they might have coveted when Mrs Gladys Ptolemy had been alive, but I think it is a fair bet that most of them were there just to look around. Since I was there only to escape from my paperwork, I was hardly in a place to criticise.

The cottage had two small rooms and a kitchen downstairs and two small bedrooms and a bathroom upstairs. At some point in the past, a modest conservatory had been built on at the back of the cottage. There was no gas supply and no central heating of any kind and the plumbing, which could best be described as rudimentary, did not stretch to indoor sanitation.

Even in her 90s, Mrs Gladys Ptolemy had still used a privy in her garden which sat above an old-fashioned cesspit. For use at night she had a chamber pot (which she always called her gazunder on the entirely reasonable grounds that it went under the bed when not in use) which had a picture of Lloyd George, a famous Victorian politician, painted onto the target area. Patchy told me that it was common for chamber pots to have many strange designs inside. One popular trick was to have an eye painted on the bottom of the pot, staring upwards in constant surprise. Another was to have a frog attempting to climb up the inside of the pot. Chamber pots were still being made as late as the 1940s when many had portraits of Adolf Hitler on the bottom. Sadly, there were several large cracks and one chip in Mrs Gladys Ptolemy's pot and despite the political decoration in the target area, Patchy said it had very little value.

I spotted a small silver box, around four inches long and no more than three inches high. I asked Patchy what it was. He told me it was a Queen Anne tea caddy.

'It's very small!' I pointed out. 'Hardly big enough to contain sufficient tea for a few pots!'

'Tea was very expensive in those days,' explained Patchy.

'Are you going to bid on it? I asked him.

'Perhaps,' he said, without much interest. 'It's the only thing I've seen so far that is worth buying,' he added.

In a cupboard, Patch found a rather elderly instrument which looked to me like a xylophone but which Patchy assured me was a glockenspiel. The difference, apparently, is that the bars on a xylophone are made of wood whereas on a glockenspiel they are made of metal. Patchy shuddered at the sight of the glockenspiel for he was no longer in the market for musical instruments. Three months ago, he bought a sousaphone, a trombone, a bassoon, a tuba and a trumpet as a job lot at an auction in South Molton. When he got them home he made the mistake of trying them all out. Adrienne, his wife and my sister-in-law, threatened to leave him if he continued or, indeed, if he bought any more musical instruments. She is a firm-minded young woman and Patchy has learned that when she says something it is best to listen carefully.

I followed Patchy around the house. It was, as always, a fascinating experience. We are all many different people. We are one person with our loved ones, another with relatives, another with friends and yet another with strangers. We constantly change, adapt, hone, refine and reinvent ourselves according to our immediate circumstances. Patchy changed completely when he was working. Back in the Duck and Puddle he was casual, carefree and light-hearted. He never seemed to take anything seriously. But when he was working, looking around an auction room or a houseful of items for sale, he became very serious and extremely focused. As a surgeon concentrates in the operating theatre, and a barrister concentrates in a court room, so Patchy concentrated in the auction room.

There was a rather decent looking Welsh dresser taking up most of the kitchen. It was made of oak but it was badly stained and damaged and would clearly need a considerable amount of restoration. The only other piece of furniture in there was an old pine table which had definitely seen better days, and two mismatching wooden chairs. The mismatched crockery lined up on the shelves of the Welsh dresser was, Patchy said, late Victorian but uninspiring and of value only for individuals who wanted to pick out a cup or a saucer or a plate to help complete a set which had been decimated by breakages.

The living room was equally disappointing.

A two seater sofa and a leather chair with the horse hair stuffing coming out of it took up most of the room. There was a small oak bookcase which was filled with old cookery books, novels by Marie Corelli and Colette and several bibles. There were a few old hunting prints on the walls, none of them particularly attractive or well framed, and a pair of fairly ordinary and uninspiring brass candlesticks on the mantelpiece. A large damp patch on the wall with the fireplace suggested that there was some serious work to be done on the fabric of the cottage.

The front room was even more disappointing than the other two rooms downstairs. It contained three easy chairs, all of which were faded and stained and had broken springs. The rugs on the floor were threadbare and probably destined for either the rubbish dump or a bonfire. There were a few knick knacks on the mantelpiece and the windowsill but none of them seemed to be of much value to anyone than a collector of seaside curios. There was an ugly looking model of a clown with the words 'A Present from Blackpool' on it. And there were similar items labelled 'A Present from Llandudno' and 'A Present from Weston-super-Mare'.

In conclusion, the rooms downstairs, small and crammed with disappointed dealers, collectors and neighbours, seemed dark and damp. Everything seemed depressing and I suddenly realised that Mrs Gladys Ptolemy must have spent the last third of her life simply marking time; unwilling or unable to improve her circumstances or her surroundings. When I had visited her, I had seen only my patient. Now, seeing the unoccupied house with Patchy, I naturally saw only the contents.

Still, Mrs Gladys Ptolemy was now gone and we were there not to mourn her passing, or to regret her failure to grasp life and squeeze the goodness out of it, but to appraise the worldly goods she had left behind.

And so we made our way up the narrow staircase to the top floor.

Upstairs was no better than downstairs.

In the main bedroom, the one which Mrs Gladys Ptolemy had used, the only item of value was the view. From the window you could see across the cottage garden, now overgrown with nettles and brambles and Giant Hogweed, over the neighbouring fields and away towards the coast. The furniture consisted of a wardrobe with a door which hung open because the catch didn't fasten properly, a double bed with a very soggy looking mattress, a stained and battered bedside table, two scruffy looking rugs and the by now customary collection of worthless bits and pieces; some of which Mrs Gladys Ptolemy had probably purchased herself and some of which had doubtless been bought for her as mementoes of other people's holidays.

There was, however, one item of interest in the room.

I doubt if I would have spotted it if I had spent half a day in the room but Patchy saw it within moments of our entering the room.

Doctors, particularly GPs, who have been in practice for a good while can often tell whether or not a patient is suffering from a serious illness the minute they see them – without examining them or doing any tests.

It is, I suppose, a matter of instinct or intuition rather than anything else. Dr Brownlow, my predecessor in Bilbury, was able to do this and occasionally I am myself aware of this sense, though I am not yet experienced enough to take full advantage of it.

Patchy has the same skill as far as antiques are concerned. In the antique dealers' world he is, because of this talent, known as a 'divvy'.

If you threw a piece of Chippendale onto a rubbish dump he would, I am sure, be able to spot it within seconds.

'What on earth is that?' I asked.

Patchy was holding a very small glass bottle. It looked a little like a small scent bottle, the sort of thing that ladies and gentlemen used to carry before baths and showers were available. They would sprinkle perfume onto their bodies and their clothes in order to mask less pleasant smells. But I didn't think it was a scent bottle. It was far too small.

'It's a Chinese tear bottle,' said Patchy, with a smile on his face.

He held up the tiny bottle so that I could see it more clearly.

'When a young Chinese man became engaged, he sent his fiancée one of these tiny glass bottles but instead of a drop of perfume it contained a tear from his eye – a tear of joy. The fiancée would treasure the gift all her life, looking after it, protecting it and making sure it didn't get broken. When her husband died, she would open up the little bottle for the first time. She would then allow a tear of her sorrow to fall into the bottle. And she would then place the tiny bottle, now containing two mingled tears, upon the breast of her dead husband before he was taken to be buried.

'Is it worth a good deal of money?' I asked him.

Patchy shook his head. 'You'd think it would be,' he said, holding up the bottle to the light. 'But there isn't much demand for them. They're rather out of fashion.' He put the bottle back down on the dressing table. 'This one has never been used,' he said. He seemed disappointed.

The second bedroom had been used as a junk room.

There was a bed in there but old bits of broken furniture were piled on top of it. There was a large, metal bound trunk in a corner with half a dozen old suitcases on top of it. The suitcases were leather and well-made but they were very battered, and Patchy said that they would require a good deal of loving attention before they could be turned into saleable pieces of luggage. 'People don't want them anyway,' he said, sadly. 'Modern luggage is lighter and easier to carry about. This sort of luggage was fine if you had servants and porters to help you carry your stuff around for you. If you took a couple of these empty cases onto a plane you would probably find yourself having to pay an excess baggage charge!'

We slowly made our way back downstairs. The cottage was still full of dealers, collectors and neighbours. Nearly all of them seemed disappointed.

'I don't understand it,' said Patchy, as we stood in the living room once more. 'I'm sure there's something here that is worthwhile. I can sense it but I can't see it.'

'Not the Chinese tear bottle?'

He shook his head.

Suddenly, he moved towards a door leading into the tiny conservatory. 'We haven't looked in here,' he said. I followed him. The conservatory was tiny and I don't think anyone else had bothered to go in. The only things in there were a small and rather unstable looking chair, made of bamboo, and a small, old table upon which stood half a dozen plant pots. The plants in the pots had not been watered and they were all dead. Patchy ignored the chair and the dead plants and went straight for the table. He bent down to take a closer look at it and then knelt beside it so that he could examine it more carefully. He took the plants off the table and placed them carefully on the conservatory floor.

I stood and watched.

The table looked to me just like the sort of scruffy old table you might expect to find being used for pot plants in a conservatory. I wouldn't have given it a second glance, or expected to pay more than a pound for it. Indeed, if I had paid a pound and taken it home with me, Patsy would have probably raised at least one eyebrow and asked me if I had been drinking.

'Is it valuable?' I asked.

Patchy stood up and gazed for a moment at the table. He then put all the plant pots back onto the table. He did this very carefully.

'Is it valuable?' I asked again.

Patchy made a shushing sound, took me by the elbow and led me out of the conservatory. He carefully closed the door behind him. I followed him back into the main part of the cottage. He then proceeded to take an extraordinary amount of interest in the small oak bookcase which he had previously ignored. Puzzled, I watched him.

I guessed that the table in the conservatory was something special but I had no idea why.

A few minutes later, when we were both strolling along the lane outside, Patchy told me about the table.

'It was made about 50 years ago by a designer called Armand-Albert Rateau,' said Patchy. He was shaking slightly with excitement. I couldn't remember ever seeing him so excited. 'Almand-Albert Rateau was one of the most exclusive and highly renowned interior decorators and furniture makers of the 1920s. The table in that conservatory is a green patinated bronze table with a marble slab top. As far as I know there is only one other similar table in the world. And the second table is in a museum in Paris: the Musee des Arts Decoratif.'

'Is it valuable?' I asked him for the third time. We were still strolling along the lane. Patchy had managed to calm himself down a little.

He looked at me. The answer to the question was now pretty obvious.

'How valuable?'

Patchy thought for a minute. 'I couldn't examine all the legs properly but there's a slight scratch on one of them,' he said. 'Assuming there are a couple more scratches that I didn't see then it's probably worth between 25 and 30.'

I was, I admit, surprised. I had thought he was going to say that it was worth a good deal.

'Oh,' I said. '£25 to £30?'

Patchy looked at me with a big smile on his face.

He shook his head.

'£25,000 to £30,000,' he said.

I stared at him.

'Heaven knows how it got here,' he added. He thought for a while. 'Maybe she inherited it or was given it or picked it up in a sale somewhere. She certainly didn't know its value.'

'Are you sure?' I asked him.

A moment ago, I'd been slightly disappointed when I'd thought the table was worth just £25 to £30. Now I was quite shocked at how valuable it was. It didn't seem quite right that such a valuable piece of furniture should be standing, unnoticed, in a conservatory, sharing life with a few plant pots.

He looked at me.

'Sorry,' I said.

'The thing is,' said Patchy, 'that I don't think anyone else has noticed it.'

'I didn't see anyone else even go into the conservatory.'

'Do you know anything about the old lady who lived there?'

I told him what I knew. By the time I had finished we were quite a distance from the cottage. A woodpecker, startled as we walked past, flew off into a small copse of beech trees. It has always surprised me that the two most nervous birds in the world seem to be the woodpecker and the jay. The woodpecker has one of the toughest beaks in the bird world and the jay is, of course, a member of the crow family. You'd expect them to be arrogant and not easily frightened but both are remarkably timid creatures. Mind you, the jay, which was once widely sought after for its feathers, has good reason to be cautious.

'Who does the money go to?' asked Patchy.

'A distant relative somewhere up in the North of England. He never came down to Devon; never visited the old lady at all. I gather that the solicitor handling the will had quite a job to find him.'

'Good,' said Patchy, looking relieved. 'That's OK then.'

I looked at him, a little puzzled.

'I'd have to tell the auctioneer if she'd left her money to a nice family in the village,' said Patchy. 'But a relative who'd never bothered to visit her is good news. I won't feel guilty about him.'

'When is the auction?' I asked.

'Tomorrow,' replied Patchy. He pulled the agent's details out of his pocket and examined them carefully. 'Yes, the auction is tomorrow.' He read on and then stopped and grinned broadly. 'Unless sold prior to auction by private treaty,' he read. He turned round and headed back for the cottage. I followed.

Ten minutes later we were standing in the back garden with Harley House, the estate agent, the man who would be auctioning the cottage and its contents on the following day.

'How much are you expecting to get for the cottage?' asked Patchy.

I could hardly believe my ears. Patchy was planning to buy the whole house in order to get the table without anyone knowing what he was doing or what they had all missed.

'The guide price is £6,000,' said the auctioneer. 'But I wouldn't sell it in advance of the sale for less than £7,000.'

'It's in terrible condition!' said Patchy. He pointed to the roof. 'The roof needs replacing, there's damp everywhere and I'm sure I could smell dry rot in the kitchen.'

The auctioneer shrugged. 'I can't sell it for less than £7,000. We could get more at the auction.'

'You could get less,' responded Patchy. 'How about £6,500?' He paused as though thinking hard. 'And I'll take all the contents off your hands. There are a couple of bits of oak that I can do something with. That'll save you the cost and trouble of auctioning the contents.'

The auctioneer thought for a moment then nodded. 'OK,' he said. '£6,500 for the house and all the contents.' They shook hands on the deal and the agent assured Patchy that nothing would be taken from the house.

And so the deal was done. I was very impressed with the speed with which it had all been conducted.

The agent went back indoors to tell all the dealers, collectors and neighbours that the cottager and the contents had all been sold and that the auction had been cancelled.

'Just like that?' I said to Patchy.

'I know the auctioneer,' said Patchy. 'He knows that the deal will be done.' He looked at his watch. 'Now I need to get into Barnstaple to go to the bank – and to see my solicitor. I'll drop you off at Bilbury Grange on the way.'

'Patchy,' I said, as we headed back to his truck, 'do you have £6,500?'

He looked at me, seemingly a little paler now. 'Not exactly at the moment,' he agreed.

'How much do you have?'

'I think there was about £20 in my current account,' he said. 'But Adrienne and I have £200 in a deposit account.' He cleared his throat. 'I've got a really nice bank manager,' he said. 'I'm sure they'll lend me the money.'

We sat in silence as we drove back towards Bilbury.

'If you mention anything to Patsy please ask her not to tell Adrienne,' said Patchy. 'I want to tell her myself when I get back from Barnstaple.'

I assured him that I would not even tell Patsy until the evening.

'I had to do it,' said Patchy, when he stopped at Bilbury Grange to drop me off. 'It's the chance of a lifetime.'

'I know you had to do it,' I said. 'And it will all work out brilliantly.'

He smiled, rather wanly. 'Let's hope so,' he said, as he disappeared towards Barnstaple.

I crossed my fingers for him. I knew I would not have had the courage to do what he had done. As I walked into the house I remembered a quote from Browning. 'A man's reach should exceed his grasp, or what's a heaven for?'

But at the time I couldn't help hoping, for his sake, that he was right about the table.

The story has a sequel.

Two weeks later Patchy came round to the house to tell me that he had managed to sell the bronze table to a London dealer for £35,000. It had truly been the deal of a lifetime.

'I've got a couple of things for you,' he said. 'Come out to the van and give me a hand.'

The couple of things he had for me were the tear bottle, which was for Patsy, and the glockenspiel. 'I daren't keep the damned thing,' he said. 'Adrienne would kill me.'

'And there's this,' said Patchy. 'It's from Adrienne and myself.'

He handed me a long white envelope.

When I opened the envelope I found a cheque for £5,000, made out to the Dr Brownlow Country Hotel Fund.

'If you hadn't come with me that day I probably wouldn't have gone to Doone Cottage,' said Patchy, when I started to protest that it was too much.

Patsy has the tear bottle on her dressing table. I've put in my tear.

I still haven't learned to play the damned glockenspiel though I'm having a good deal of fun learning.

The Chimney Sweep's Tattoo

I don't think there is a house or cottage in Bilbury which doesn't have an open fireplace.

Houses in towns and cities are all equipped with central heating these days but in our part of North Devon, central heating is still something of a rarity. Most people keep their houses warm by throwing logs or coal onto a fire or into a stove. Since wood is readily available, and is usually either free or very cheap, it is the fuel of choice.

The one snag with relying on an open fire is, of course, the very real need to have the chimney swept once or twice a year. When you live three quarters of an hour away from a fire station, it's a good idea to cut down the chance of having a chimney fire.

At Bilbury Grange we have a number of fireplaces and although Patsy and I don't use the one in our bedroom very often, we always like to have at least three chimneys swept regularly. When you burn wood rather than coal there is a tendency for large amounts of resinous substances to be deposited inside the chimney.

For years we, and most other villages, relied on a man called Bill Rattenbury to sweep our chimneys. And when Bill retired a year or so ago we transferred our allegiance to his son, Jack, who had worked with him, learning the tricks of the trade and the idiosyncrasies of local chimneys, for several years. Many sweeps are starting to use vacuum cleaners to remove the soot out of chimneys but both Bill and Jack have always relied on their brushes.

A good sweep can help in many ways – not just cleaning the soot out of the chimney. The Rattenburys have given us lots of good advice. To get a good draught in any sort of chimney it is necessary to have a substantial temperature difference between the gas inside the chimney and the outside air. As any child knows, hot air rises and if there is plenty of heat at the bottom of the chimney then the air will rise upwards and create a good draught. If a fireplace is too large, and the bottom part of a chimney too wide, then there will be too much cold air from the room going into the chimney and the fire won't draw properly. The Rattenburys helped us with several of our fireplaces; adjusting the size of one, putting a new chimney pot on another and simply raising the fire basket on a third.

However, when I telephoned Jack a month ago, to arrange an appointment for him to come round and do the necessary, I had quite a shock. Jack told me that he couldn't sweep our chimneys for nearly month and that he was considering retiring from the chimney sweeping business. This was bad news. There are two other sweeps in the area and while one of them is very grumpy and has a reputation for leaving behind quite a mess, the other is 83-years-old and said to be contemplating what he describes as 'early retirement'. The grumpy one isn't even a professional chimney sweep. He has what he calls a portfolio of jobs and when he isn't sweeping chimneys he can be found driving a taxi, taking wedding photographs or doing a little French polishing. I've heard it said that he also does a little light embalming – not to mention an occasional bout of poaching.

'Why on earth are you retiring?' I asked him when he turned up.

'I've started doing weddings,' he told me. 'There's quite a market.'

He explained that a lot of brides still thought it was good luck to have a chimney sweep turn up at their weddings. He said all he had to do was stand and pose next to the bride (possibly giving her a slightly sooty kiss on the cheek but taking great care not to get soot on her dress) and that he could charge £15 to turn up at a wedding. Since Jack charges £3 to sweep a chimney (and £2 more for each additional chimney in a house) I could see his point.

'They often give me a bottle of wine or champagne,' he said, 'and they nearly always invite me to have a bit to eat with them.' He paused. 'I always have them bring my food out to me, though,' he said, 'and eat it outside or in the van if it's raining.'

'That's very thoughtful of you,' I said.

'Soot can be very difficult to remove,' he explained.

'And there are other perks,' he added. 'There are always bridesmaids with romantic ideas foremost in their minds.' He grinned.

'I suppose there would be,' I agreed.

'I'm thinking of taking out an advertisement in one of those magazines for brides,' he said. 'This could be quite a business opportunity for me.'

I had to agree with him that it seemed as though he might have hit upon an excellent money making idea. But I told him that Patsy and I, and the rest of the village, would miss his services as a chimney sweep.

'Oh don't worry, doctor,' he said, 'I'll always be available to pop round and do your chimneys.'

I said that was very good of him and that I hoped he would keep a few days a month free to sweep chimneys for some of the other villagers – especially the older folk.

He said he would do that and that he would need a constant supply of soot to put onto his face and hands when attending weddings. Then, hesitantly, asked me if he could consult me as a patient. I said that of course he could.

To be honest, I'm fairly accustomed to workmen suddenly stripping off and showing me their bits and pieces. Not long ago a carpenter who was doing some work on our front porch suddenly pulled down his trousers to show me his hernia. He wasn't a patient of mine and didn't live in the village but he wanted a second opinion. Patsy came outside to ask him if he wanted a cup of tea just as he was displaying his large lump and it was, I think, the first time I've seen her blush quite such a deep shade of red. Patsy said afterwards that it was a good job that Miss Johnson, a committed maiden lady, had not chosen that moment to leave the house. Curiously, I remember, the man wore boxer shorts emblazoned with small pictures of fire engines.

Jack told me that he had a tattoo he wanted removing.

I said I'd better take a look.

'I think I'd perhaps better undress outside,' said Jack, looking down at the carpet. He and his clothes were, as usual, thick with soot.

'Where's the tattoo?' I asked.

'On my arm.'

'OK, then if you don't mind it might be a good idea if you popped out into the garden.' I didn't mind him taking his shirt off in the garden, but I knew darned well that if he removed his trousers someone would choose that moment to turn up to deliver a parcel or collect some plants from the small market garden which our gardener helps run for us.

I opened the French windows which lead out from my consulting room and we stepped outside. Jack unbuttoned and then removed his shirt and, to be honest, I was grateful that he was doing this in the garden. The cloud of soot would have taken some cleaning up. 'I always get undressed in the garden,' said Jack, who still lives at home, 'and my mum then throws a couple of cold buckets of water over me. She always did that for my Dad.'

I shivered at the thought.

'Quite refreshing,' said Jack.

'I bet it is,' I said.

He showed me the tattoo. It wasn't difficult to spot. The skin over his left biceps was tattooed with the name 'Doreen'. The letters had been done in blue and red ink and there were roses entwined around the letters.

Tattoos can look decorative on a young body but I often wonder what the owners will feel when they are in their 80s and their skin is decorated with faded and barely legible ink.

'Can you remove it?' he asked, nervously.

I guessed immediately what had happened.

A cosmetic surgeon I know once told me that there were two simple rules about tattoos; first, that no one should ever have themselves tattooed when drunk and second that no one should ever have themselves tattooed with the name of a lover they had known for less than three decades.

'You and Doreen have split up?'

He nodded. 'She was two timing me with a scaffolder from South Molton.'

I examined the tattoo, then told him he could put his shirt back on and come back into the surgery.

'It's not something I can do here in Bilbury,' I told him.

Our own small centre of medical excellence, known for administrative reasons as The Brownlow Country Hotel, is designed more for providing simple nursing care rather than anything else and although I don't mind attending to a small varicose vein or removing an occasional mole, skin tag or lipoma, I was confident that removing an entire tattoo was well outside my modest range of surgical skills.

'Removing a tattoo is never easy to do,' I went on. 'But I can fix up an appointment for you to see a cosmetic surgeon. They've developed some techniques for removing tattoos and he'll be able to tell you what's possible and what's not possible.'

Jack nodded again. I wasn't sure whether he was shy or merely embarrassed.

'You may have to go to Exeter to get it removed,' I said. 'Or even to Bristol.'

'That's OK,' he said.

When he'd gone, I wrote a note to a cosmetic surgeon who has a clinic once a week. The cosmetic surgeon deals with breasts which their owners think too small or too large, with ears that stick out like jug handles and with noses which did not please their owners. He had also, so I had heard, acquired some experience in the delicate and tricky art of removing tattoos. His bedside manner is, to be honest, something of an acquired taste (a colleague of his once told me that he had gone to the Captain Bligh School of Diplomacy) but he is the only cosmetic surgeon available.

To my surprise Jack, the young man with a tattoo surplus to requirements, was back in my surgery a couple of weeks later.

'I've written to the hospital,' I told him, assuming that he'd come to complain that he hadn't yet received an appointment, 'but I'm afraid it will take a while for them to get back to you. There's quite a queue for cosmetic surgery these days.'

'It's OK,' he said, waving a hand, 'you don't have to do anything. I just came to tell you that I don't want my tattoo removed.'

'Ah,' I said, 'you've made up with the girl?'

'Oh no,' he said with a shudder. 'That's properly over.'

Jack looked down at the floor, as though wondering how to say what he clearly needed to say. I wondered for a moment if he'd somehow managed to find a tattoo artist able to convert 'Doreen' into something else; 'Noreen' or 'Doris' or, somehow, 'Mother'. Or maybe someone had found a way to turn 'Doreen' into a three masted schooner or a howling wolf. I once saw a young lady who had five tattoos on her left arm. All were the names of lovers but the first four names on the list had a neat, horizontal line tattooed through them. The girl concerned was only 19-years-old when I saw her and I couldn't help wondering if she would have enough space on her body for a lifetime of crossed out names.

'I've met someone else,' said Jack suddenly. 'I met her at a wedding in Barnstaple a week last Saturday. I was there to kiss the bride and pose for a few photographs and she was one of the bridesmaids.'

'And she doesn't mind the tattoo?'

'Oh no,' said the young man. 'She's a prim and proper girl and she hasn't actually seen it yet. But when she does I know she won't mind. In fact I think she'll like it.'

I looked at him and frowned. I found this difficult to believe.

'Her name's Doreen,' explained the young man. 'She'll think I've had it done for her. And she's bound to think it's dead romantic. Don't you think?'

'I suppose that's a possibility,' I said. 'But are you sure this relationship is going to last?'

'Dunno yet, do I?' said the young man. 'But I thought about it quite a bit and I think I'll keep the tattoo anyway.'

'Right,' I said, 'that's good.'

'Because even if this girl and I don't hit it off, I can always find another Doreen can't I?'

I looked at him.

'There are thousands of girls called Doreen,' he explained. 'I'm bound to be able to find a girl called Doreen to settle down with.'

'I suppose so,' I agreed.

Jack stood up and smiled. 'So you can cancel that appointment,' he said.

'It seems as if your new business has brought you love as well as a good income,' I said, as he headed for the door.

He turned and grinned.

'Doreen wants me to give up the weddings,' he said, 'she says she'll always be worried that I'm going to pick up another bridesmaid.'

'So you're going to concentrate on sweeping chimneys?' I asked.

'It was good enough for my Dad,' said Jack. 'So I guess it'll do for me.' He paused, his hand on the doorknob. 'To be honest with you,' he said, 'I was getting a bit fed up with all the travelling. And then there's the problem of the soot.'

'The soot?'

'The wedding parties always expect you to turn up covered in soot,' he explained. 'And I can only get sooty if I sweep chimneys, can't I?' He sighed. 'And travelling round the country covered in soot isn't much fun. I had to go down to Torquay a week or so ago and when I stopped off at a café for a cup of tea they turned me away – said I'd mess up their furniture.'

The collapse of his new career venture may have been slightly disappointing for Jack but it was, I confess, good news for Patsy and me. And I suspected that the rest of the village would be pleased to hear that we'd got our chimney sweep back.

When Jack had gone, I rang the hospital, got in touch with the secretary who handles appointments for the cosmetic surgeon, and told her to toss my letter into the circular filing cabinet underneath her desk.

'The patient has changed his mind,' I told her. 'He's going to keep his tattoo.'

'Oh right,' said the secretary. 'Do you know what the tattoo is? You didn't say in your letter.'

An alarm bell rang somewhere at the back of my head.

'I'm not entirely sure,' I mumbled. 'Can't quite remember now...'

'Oh,' said the secretary, a trifle disappointed. 'Okay. I expect we'll see it in due course. It's just that he's started going out with my daughter, Doreen. They met at a wedding recently. He seems a nice young man.'

I made a note to ring Jack. I am confident he'll find a convincing explanation.

The Doc's Bad Back

It was my own darned fault.

I have lost count of the number of times I've told people that they must be careful when lifting anything heavy, and that they should always take care to lift with their knees bent and their back straight.

But we don't always do what we know what we should do, or what we tell other people they should do.

An old beech tree of ours came down in last winter's most ferocious gale and Thumper Robinson used his chainsaw to chop up the trunk and the main branches into suitable lengths for burning in our fireplace. Chainsaws terrify me and I'd taken on the far less hazardous task of cutting up the smaller branches into kindling.

As Thumper did the cutting, I moved the logs into the old stable where we store our cut wood. This simply meant picking up the logs, putting them into the wheelbarrow and wheeling them to the stable.

It was during the picking up phase that I had become lazy, and had done the lifting with my back bent. When I woke up the following morning, I knew instantly that I was in trouble. My back was as stiff as a board and it hurt like the devil to try to move. The good news was that I was pretty sure that I hadn't slipped a disk or done any serious damage. I had no pains down the backs of my legs and no pains in my feet. But I had back muscles that were tense, inflamed and sore and screaming to be allowed to stay exactly where they were for a while. I tried several times to get out of bed but every attempt ended in yelps of pain. In the end, I managed to slide out of bed and shuffle along to the bathroom just a few yards away but I knew that I would not be able to dress myself, go down the stairs, sit in a chair or drive the car.

'It's no good. I'm going to have to stay in bed for a day or two,' I told Patsy eventually. 'It isn't serious but I literally can't get up.'

'What do you want to do about the patients?' she asked.

Suddenly I came face to face with the nightmare that always awaits everyone who works for themselves and who has no partners, associates or employees to stand in for them. It was my first day's illness since Dr Brownlow had retired and I knew that I was lucky to have managed so far without needing to find another doctor to help look after the practice.

'You'll find the telephone number of a locum agency in my desk diary,' I told her. 'Ring them please, and see if they can provide us with a locum for a couple of days.'

Ten minutes later Patsy was back.

'They can't provide a locum until next week,' she said. 'And then they can only provide one for a whole week. They don't do odd days.'

I swore quietly. I very much enjoyed working as a single-handed practitioner but at that moment I would have happily swapped my life with one of my medical friends working in large practices. I knew that when they were ill they simply took some time off, knowing that their partners and assistants would take over their work. The single-handed practitioner, particularly in the country, has no such luxury.

'Hopefully, I'll be better by then,' I said.

'I could ring around the local practices to see if anyone can help out,' suggested Patsy.

'Good idea!'

I lay in bed, unmoving. I knew that my friend William, who works in a large practice and has numerous partners, would come down and help out for a few days, but to do so he would have to take some holiday from his own practice. I really didn't want to ask him to do that.

I hated being ill. Outside I could hear the lesser spotted woodpecker hammering on the silver birch tree which stands beside our bedroom. No one works harder than a woodpecker: constantly busy. I remembered that I had read somewhere that a woodpecker bangs his beak into a tree 12,000 times a day, with each bang producing a G force of 1,000.

I tried to read, holding a book above my head, but after a couple of minutes my arms hurt so much that I had to lower the book. Ben, our faithful canine friend, who had been lying on the floor leapt up onto the bed but, sensing that all was not well, kept to the bottom of the bed by my feet.

Twenty minutes later, Patsy returned.

'I've tried all the local doctors,' she said, 'and Dr Middleton in Chugborough says you can give patients his number if it's a genuine emergency. But he can't cover your surgeries because he's got his own to do. Nor can anyone else I'm afraid. Apparently there is an epidemic of gastrointestinal poisoning in Combe Martin and the doctors there are rushed off their feet.'

'Are there any patients in the waiting room?' I asked. I looked at the clock. It was ten minutes to ten. The morning surgery was already nearly an hour late.

'Five,' said Patsy. 'There were twelve but the other seven said they'd come back another day. And there are half a dozen requests for repeat prescriptions. Two people rang asking you to visit them at home but when I explained that you were poorly in bed they said they would ring back in a couple of days to see how you were. They said it wasn't urgent. Everyone said they were sorry to hear you were bad and hoped you'd get well soon.'

'If you bring me a prescription pad I can write out the prescriptions,' I said. 'But I don't have the foggiest idea what we're going to do with the five patients in the surgery.'

'You definitely can't get downstairs?'

I shook my head.

'Then we'll have to bring the patients up here!' said Patsy brightly. 'If Mohammed can't go to the mountains then the mountains must come to Mohammed!' She busied herself around the room moving bits of clothing and personal items out of sight. She helped me put on a shirt and she put a tie around my neck. Below the waist, hidden from view, I was still wearing pyjama trousers. Above the waist I did at least look respectable. She put a chair beside the bed, for patients to sit on, and then hunted around in the back of our wardrobe until she found a large wooden tray with legs. This made a splendid, temporary desk on top of the bedclothes. She put a prescription pad on the table and then fetched my stethoscope, auriscope, opthalmoscope and sphygmomanometer and, having moved aside the alarm clock, the bedside lamp and the book I had been reading the night before she put all the medical paraphernalia on the table at my side of the bed.

'Ready?' she said, at last.

'Just about,' I agreed.

'Can you sit up a bit higher?' she asked.

'I'm afraid not,' I said with a sigh. I was lying almost flat, with just one pillow under my head. When I tried to sit up a little higher the pain in my back got worse. I had really given my back muscles a hard time and now they were definitely making me pay for my stupidity. They were, you might say, getting their own back.

'Shall I get tell the first patient to come up?' said Patsy.

'OK,' I sighed.

Patsy took one last look around the bedroom, spotted a small pile of freshly laundered, neatly folded underwear on a chair and stuffed the lot into a drawer in the dressing table. And then she went back downstairs to tell the patient who had been first into the waiting room that morning to come up and see me.

'Sorry to see you in bed,' said Mr Daglingpole Birdlip. 'Your wife says you have a bad back.' Miss Johnson, my receptionist, had given him his medical records envelope to bring upstairs with him and he put the envelope down on top of the bedclothes, just out of my reach. I could immediately see that the conjunctiva of his right eye was almost completely red.

I agreed that the information he had been given was entirely accurate and that I did, indeed, have a bad back. I could, to be honest, have hoped for a better start to a difficult surgery.

Mr Birdlip is a strange and indomitably gloomy fellow, though he is possibly not as strange as his father who was, for a variety of reasons, something of a local legend. The family has for centuries lived in a large house near Blackmoor Gate. Their ancestors are reputed to have made their money out of smuggling, which was once a very common and profitable activity along the North Devon coast. They were, so it is rumoured, also heavily involved in selling opium to the Chinese and doing a little slave trading.

Sixty or seventy years ago, the Birdlips were rich enough to have servants and in cold weather Mr P's father would call for a servant to act as a human hot water bottle. In those days, maids regarded the chore of being taken to bed by their employer as being as much a part of their domestic duties as laying a fire in the drawing room but old Mr P was different in that his requirements were not for a sexual partner but for someone to keep him warm – a human hot water bottle.

According to legend, he didn't much care which servant offered themselves for this activity, though he preferred the plumper variety of servant since he believed that they produced the most heat. Patchy, who knows a good deal of local history, and even more scurrilous gossip, says that the various male members of staff were as likely as the most luscious junior scullery maid to be selected. Towards the end of Mr Birdlip's days, the servants would cut cards for the post which was coveted, for although no sexual activity was offered or expected, a fee of one guinea was always paid in cash when the morning breakfast tray was delivered and the human hot water bottle discharged from their duties.

Sadly, for the current Mr Birdlip, the money and the big house had gone.

Mr Birdlip's father had made a single disastrous investment in a small company which had supposedly found large quantities of gold and silver somewhere in Africa. Unfortunately, the only gold and silver in the mine was the stuff which had been put there to 'salt the mine' by the trickster who had founded the company.

After the old man's death, the young Birdlip had to sell the house to pay off his father's debts. He had been left with very little and had taken a job as a labourer on a neighbouring farm. Ever since I have known him, he has struggled through life with a chip the size of a telegraph pole resting on his shoulder. And for most of that time he has been attempting to give up his smoking habit (sixty of the cheapest and most toxic cigarettes it is possible to buy) and his drinking habit (eight or ten pints a night at a small table for one in the Duck and Puddle).

Lean and lugubrious, he has worked outside all his adult life and his skin had been so well weathered that it is impossible to guess at his age other than to say that he was adult somewhere between the ages of 40 and 80. He is, in fact, still in his early 40s.

And, oddly, despite his smoking and his drinking, he is a world-class hypochondriac. If they gave out medals for introspection and hypochondriasis he would have a drawer full of the damned things. I'm prepared to wager that he knows more about medical matters than some professionals. Smoking and drinking are his habits. His hobby is medicine and crammed into the tiny cottage which he rents, he has a medical library which most doctors would envy.

Whenever he has a day off (once a week) or a holiday (two weeks a year, not to be taken consecutively or in the harvest season) he spends it visiting bookshops and second-hand shops in search of more medical volumes to add to his collection. His problem (and occasionally my problem) is that whenever he has any unusual signs or symptoms he flicks through his books and finds the gloomiest of all possible explanations. He has had cancer seven times in the last couple of years alone (bone cancer, skin cancer, stomach cancer, oesophageal cancer, brain cancer, liver cancer and kidney cancer). In each case there was a very simple explanation for his condition.

A year or two ago he bought himself a second-hand sphygmomanometer and a second-hand stethoscope and used them to take his blood pressure.

I eventually confiscated them both after he had rung me one Sunday evening at 10 p.m. to tell me that he thought he was about to die.

'I've got no blood pressure!' he said. 'I expect I'll be dead by the time you get here.'

I raced round to his cottage and found him pale and shaking. I took his blood pressure and it was, as usual, 115/80. 'There's nothing wrong with your blood pressure,' I told him. 'It's better than mine. And you're definitely not dying.'

I examined his sphygmomanometer which looked as it had probably been new back in the days of the First World War, when such machines were first becoming widely available.

'You're healthy, but the rubber bulb in your sphygmomanometer has sprung a leak,' I told him. 'Where on earth did you find this thing?'

'I bought it in a house sale in Taunton,' he told me, 'it used to belong to a doctor.' He announced this as though the ownership of the machine had bestowed upon it an air of infallibility.

'You're fine,' I told him. 'But the sphygmomanometer has died.'

By then the pallor and the shaking had both stopped.

Inevitably, by the time I got back home, a film which I'd been looking forward to all week had finished. It was my own fault for planning to watch a film being shown on television rather than a video which I could turn on and off. Patsy assured me that it had been very good and that she would endeavour to purchase a copy next time she went into Barnstaple.

'I had a bad back once,' said Mr Birdlip, who was still beside my bed and who was standing staring down at me as though he were an undertaker and I were a prospect. 'It was a terrible thing. It went on for months and months.' He pursed his lips and shook his head.

'I'm sorry to hear that,' I said.

'Awful pain,' he said. 'I couldn't move an inch. After a couple of weeks I felt quite suicidal.'

'Ah,' I said. This was definitely not making me feel any more cheerful.

'I knew a bloke who spent five years in bed with a bad back,' said Mr Birdlip. 'In the end he lost the use of everything below his waist – legs, whatnot and all. His wife got fed up and left him.' He nodded thoughtfully. 'Can't blame her really, can you? She ended up nursing him, you see. And with him not having any feeling in his whatnot, there was no chance at all of any marital conjugations.'

The full-blooded hypochondriac always has a new complaint, a new disease to talk about. And most hypochondriacs are persistently gloomy. Mr Birdlip is no exception. I always try to be sympathetic and understanding but I really didn't want to hear any more gloomy stuff about bad backs.

I have done quite an amount of research into hypochondriasis over the years for I have several hypochondriacs among my patients. The term 'hypochondria' was first used in its modern sense in the 17th century when it was used to describe a form of depression that was accompanied by rather vague pains and general bowel problems. Leeches were usually the favoured method of treatment. In England, the disorder became rather chic. It was known to its sufferers as 'hyp' and the anxiety and gloom that accompanied it were generally regarded as a sign of intelligence. Most sufferers from 'hyp' were male (Samuel Johnson and James Boswell were both sufferers) and women with similar symptoms were usually said to be suffering from 'hysteria' – then regarded as the female equivalent of 'hyp'.

In the 18th and 19th centuries, doctors stoked the fires of hypochondria by constantly discovering new diseases and telling people about them. Proust wrote that 'For each illness that doctors cure with medicine, they provoke ten in healthy people by inoculating them with the virus that is a thousand times more powerful than any microbe: the idea that one is ill.'

Sigmund Freud, the sex-obsessed Austrian, dismissed the whole thing (arguing, inevitably, that hypochondria was merely the result of misplaced sexual urges) but hypochondriasis has steadily become increasingly common and a bigger and bigger problem for doctors. The big danger, of course, is that the doctor may be tempted to dismiss the fears of a patient who is a known hypochondriac, even when they present with signs or symptoms which are, or could be, indications of some serious disorder.

'What's your problem today?' I asked him, not wanting to hear any more of his reminiscences about back problems.

'I've got leukaemia, doctor,' he announced, with surprising levity. 'I doubt if I've got many more months to live.' He made this announcement calmly and without regret or sadness; as though it were his inevitable destiny. He rubbed his fingers through the hair he no longer had. It was, I suspect, a gesture he had done many times when he was younger. Now, he still made the gesture but the hair had almost all gone. Mr Birdlip suffers from premature male pattern baldness. I suspect that worrying about his health has probably expedited the hair loss.

I looked up at him, puzzled. 'Won't you sit down? There's a chair there you can use.' I pointed to the chair that Patsy had positioned for patients to use.

'I'd rather stand,' he said. 'For as long as I am able.'

'What makes you think you have leukaemia?' I asked him. I found looking at him very difficult and quite uncomfortable.

'The bleed in the conjunctiva,' he said. 'My books say it happens with leukemia. The growth in the number of white cells is inevitably accompanied by a shortage of platelets. And the absence of platelets means an increased likelihood of bleeding.' He sighed; the deep dark sigh of a man who has prepared himself to face the ferryman of Hades. 'Has it occurred to you,' he continued, 'that one can be bouncing along without a care in the world, full of beans and bursting with joie de vivre, and then you get up one morning and you have a spot or a cough or a numb bit of skin or, in my case, a red eye, and you think nothing of it and then bang, 24 hours later you're on your back in an ambulance and 48 hours after that you're on a slab in the morgue with a scar from here to eternity and the top of your skull held on with staples?' He paused and laughed. It was one of those laughs usually described as 'hollow'. 'And people say not to worry!'

'Well, when you put it like that…'

115

'I do. Indeed I do put it just like that. I have lived hour by hour, always watchful and never taking tomorrow for granted. We are all of us so close to disaster – always just moments away from some terrible end. A seemingly innocuous symptom can be the harbinger of death. You can be meandering along, blissfully happy, and suddenly life will pop you on the head and it's all over.'

I looked up at him and heard myself sighing. 'I suppose so,' I muttered.

'They do fasten the top of the skull back on with staples don't they? When they've cut it off so that they can examine the brain. Or do they glue it back on? So that the corpse looks good in the coffin.'

I hesitated. 'I'm not entirely sure,' I admitted. 'Almost certainly not glue.' I looked up at his eye. 'Have you ever had anything like it before?'

Even when I am feeling well, and on top of my form, I find Mr Birdlip to be rather hard work.

'Never,' said Mr Birdlip firmly. 'Not once in 42 years.' He thought for a moment. 'No, I tell a lie. I had a bleed when I was hit in the eye by a tennis ball. But that was a traumatically induced conjunctival haemorrhage.' He paused and sighed. 'This time I definitely haven't been hit in the eye by a tennis ball. I haven't seen a tennis ball for 30 years.'

'Do you get hay fever?' I asked.

He shook his head. He still hadn't sat down. I was getting a stiff neck looking up at him.

'Have you had flu? A cold? Anything that made you sneeze?'

'No,' he said. 'I take my vitamins every day.'

'Have you been rubbing your eyes? Dust in them?'

Another shake of the head.

'Have you been lifting anything heavy?'

'Oh yes, doctor. We had a delivery of feed and the forklift truck broke down. I had to unload it all by hand. I've got a hernia but I didn't mention that since there is no point really, is there?'

'Why is there no point?'

'Well, the leukaemia will kill me before I could have the hernia repaired, won't it?'

'Let me look at the hernia,' I told him.

He unfastened his trousers. I could immediately see that he had a right sided inguinal hernia. I see a lot of hernias in my practice since many of my patients lift things for a living.

'Turn your head and cough,' I said.

'Why do you want me to turn my head?' He asked. 'Does that make a difference to what happens to the hernia?'

'No. But it means you won't cough in my face.'

'Ah!'

He turned his head and coughed. I could see the hernia grow larger as the pressure in his abdomen increased.

'Did the hernia develop after you'd been unloading the bags of feed?'

'It did, doctor.'

'And you had the conjunctival bleed at the same time?'

'I did, doctor.'

'They're connected,' I told him. 'They were both caused by the fact that you were lifting something very heavy. You've got Ebers Disease.'

An inguinal hernia isn't usually referred to by that name but I knew that if I told Mr Birdlip that he had a common or garden hernia he would be devastated. So I told him he had Ebers Disease since I remembered being told by one of my lecturers at medical school that the first recorded description of a hernia appeared in an Egyptian papyrus on medical matters. The papyrus, which first appeared around 1500 BC was known as the Ebers Papyrus.

'I've got what?'

'Ebers disease!'

He looked puzzled. 'Who's got my disease then?' he demanded. It took me a moment to realise that in his confusion and mild paranoia he was now assuming that there had been another medical screw up and that while he had Ebers disease there was another patient running around somewhere suffering from Birdlip disease. He is a rather humourless man who tends to take everything literally. Life with Mr Birdlip is not easy and I long ago realised why he remains a bachelor.

'No, no,' I protested. 'You've got Ebers disease. That's the technical term.'

I told him that the blood on his conjunctiva would disappear over the next few days. 'And I'll arrange for you to see a surgeon about that hernia, the Ebers disease' I told him. 'Meanwhile I'll prescribe a truss and you'd better not do any heavy lifting.'

'What about the leukaemia? How long do you think I've got?'

'You haven't got leukaemia,' I told him.

He looked at me. 'Are you sure?'

I looked at him sternly. 'Who is the doctor here?'

'Oh, you are. Definitely,' said Mr Birdlip. He suddenly brightened up. 'It was just the lifting then?'

'It was just the lifting,' I told him. I didn't tell him I thought he was lucky to get away with a hernia rather than a crippling back pain.

My second patient was a woman from the Badgworthy Valley called Betty Rutter.

In contrast to Mr Birdlip, Betty Rutter is a constantly bright and jolly woman who is prone to bursting into giggles for no discernible reason. She once told me that a woman's place is in the bedroom and nowhere else. Her husband does the cooking every evening when he comes in from the fields. She does not believe in housework and so, as a result, every surface in their farmhouse is covered in a generous layer of dust. It is said that household dust is made up largely of skin cells and if that is truly the case then there is now probably enough dust in their house to recreate an army of giants.

'Do you mind if I shut the door, doctor?' asked Mrs Rutter. She lowered her voice. 'It's a bit personal, you see.'

'Of course not,' I said.

There was silence for a moment and then although I could not see what was happening I could hear her struggling to close the door.

Bilbury Grange is an old house and, like older people, it has a good many idiosyncrasies. The back door can only be unlocked if you pull up on the handle when you turn the key. Fortunately, since we hardly ever lock any of our doors this doesn't matter much. The door to the butler's pantry won't open unless you pull the handle down and inwards at the same time. The front door won't open or shut unless you pull the door towards you. And our bedroom door also requires special attention.

'You need to push the door in with your left knee and then with your right hand pull up the doorknob. Then it will close.'

There were sounds of much scuffling and pushing, pulling and panting. Eventually, there was a sound of the door clicking shut.

'Done it,' said Mrs Rutter. She suddenly burst into giggles. 'What would folk say?' she asked.

'Say about what?' I asked.

'If they knew you and I were shut in your bedroom together!'

'I don't think there's any danger of anything improper occurring,' I said. I realised when I'd said it that it sounded rather pompous.

She sat by the bed in silence for a while. I waited. Eventually I asked her if she had come to see me for any particular reason.

She laughed, as though this were very funny. 'I went into Barnstaple the other week and quite forgot what I'd gone for,' she told me. 'Things like that happen to me all the time. I do remember some things quite vividly but I'm not always entirely convinced that I manage to put them in the correct order or the proper context or indeed whether the things I do remember actually happened or whether I just imagined them.'

I made a reassuring and encouraging sound. It is a sound all GPs acquire as they become more experienced. It is a sound which means 'Please go on'. It is often said that you can safely tell a GP anything since he or she will know too much to be shocked or even surprised. This is true but conversations with Mrs Rutter always left me slightly discombobulated; as though I'd had slightly too much to drink and was no longer quite sure what was going on.

'I've got a little lump,' she said. She stood up, pulled her skirt up as far as it would go and then pulled her voluminous knee length knickers down. The knickers were of the bloomers style which used to be popular with Victorian lady cyclists. She then pointed to a scar on her abdomen. There was, indeed, a small lump at the site of the scar. It occurred to me that if I had been playing 'patient bingo' I would be doing well. I had scored two hernias in a row.

'What was the operation for?' I asked.

'Oh, I don't know,' she answered. 'I think they took something away.'

'Don't you know what it was that they removed?'

'Oh good heavens no!' she said, quite firmly. 'I didn't like to ask.' She paused and looked at me. 'It wouldn't have been polite would it?'

'That's OK,' I said, 'you can put your skirt back down now.'

'They know what they're doing, don't they? Or at least we have to assume they know what they're doing, don't we?'

'I guess so,' I agreed. I liked it that she included me with her. I always think a good GP should always be on the side of the patients. If it's going to be 'us versus them' then I need to be on the 'us' team with the patients.

'And shall I pull up my knickers?'

Mrs Rutter is a very precise woman.

'Indeed. Absolutely. You should pull up your knickers too.'

This was more of a struggle than it would have been if she had done it before she had allowed her ankle length skirt to fall back into position.

'I'll write to the hospital and arrange for you to see a surgeon,' I told her. I wondered idly if I could get a special deal from the hospital. Have one hernia repaired, get the other repaired free.

It took her some time but Mrs Rutter eventually managed to get the door open. She was giggling loudly when she left.

The third patient that morning was Tiggy Marwood.

Tiggy has had five children with five different fathers and I am still waiting for her to learn that babies are like promises in that they are very easy to make but much harder to keep.

She had started her career in motherhood at the age of 16 which was, when she began, quite an early age. 'Virginity is very overrated,' she once told me. 'It's like a balloon. One prick and it's gone forever.'

Tiggy had been born in London where her mother, Lilian Marwood, had been a professional 'knocker up' in the 1930s.

I'd never heard of this sort of employment before but it seemed that her mother's job required her to wake her clients every morning by blowing dried peas at their bedroom windows. She had to get up at 4.00 a.m. and was finished work by 6.30 a.m. She used a small wooden tube for firing the peas, clearly a piece of professional pea-shooting equipment, and the job had been handed down in her family for three generations. I gather that the business had been pretty well destroyed by alarm clocks and when the business died on the outbreak of the Second World War Mrs Marwood had less than fifty clients. I met Lilian Marwood once when she came to Bilbury for a few days. She suffered from thyrotoxicosis, refused to contemplate treatment and I suspect that she never weighed more than seven stones fully clothed in winter.

Tiggy is an unusual woman. Every time I see her she tells me that her best pal is serving five years in Exeter jail for soliciting and that she once lived next door to a woman whose son played professional football for Hartlepool United. I don't know why she tells me these things but I suspect that she thinks I will, in some way, be impressed.

Tiggy has an exceptional talent for saying the wrong thing at the wrong time to the wrong person. I think she probably always means well, but has a bad case of 'foot in mouth disease' and is a specialist in the unintentional backhanded compliment. I once heard her say to a villager who was wearing a new dress: 'That's a very nice dress. Did you make it yourself?' And I heard her say to a fellow who was showing off a lovely new car which he had been saving up to buy for several months: 'Did you inherit some money?' None of this was said to hurt but these, and many other, unfortunate incidents mean that people sometimes find themselves busy examining a hedge or looking down at the ground if they see Tiggy out and about in the village.

She was, she told me, now pregnant again and had decided that this time she wanted her latest paramour to be present in the bedroom at the birth of their child. She said she'd read a magazine article about women whose husbands had been in the labour room with them. Apparently, they all said that it had strengthened their relationships. 'They say that since the man was there at the going in bit of the pregnancy, it is only right that he should be there at the coming out bit.'

I didn't tell Tiggy but I was not quite so enthusiastic about the current enthusiasm for encouraging all fathers to be in the delivery room at the moment of truth. Some are probably better suited to pacing up and down in the corridor outside. The delivery room can be messy, noisy and unnerving. I fear that a nervous father to be might end up feeling nauseous and guilty – as well as considering himself to be somewhat surplus to requirements.

I said I would be happy for him to be present. But that he would have to leave the bedroom if he felt sick or thought he might faint.

Tiggy was delighted. But I had real reservations. When she told me his name, I realised that I knew her current lover. Nigel is a patient of mine. He is a nice enough fellow, a very nervous unemployed male model, and to be honest I had always thought of him as 'batting for the other side', as I have heard it described.

Actually, he calls himself a male model but I don't think he has ever done any modelling. I remember he told me that he thought he would make a good model because he has never had any difficulty in moving around while wearing clothes and felt, indeed, that he was very good at it. I told him, rather tentatively, that I thought there might be more to it than that but he insisted that there is not.

'You don't have a hernia, by any chance, do you?' I asked Tiggy, as she headed for the door. She turned and looked at me, frowning slightly. 'A hernia? No, I don't think so. Why? Should I?'

'No, no, it's nothing,' I said. 'It's just that we're running a special offer on hernias today.'

She left, looking very confused.

My fourth patient that day was Lord Chilcott who is, to be frank, not quite what he might seem to be. He lives in East Ilkerton but insists on staying on my list of patients because he says I understand him in a way that no other doctor possibly could or would.

His surname is Chilcottt and his Christian name is Lord, in the same way that Mr Ellington's first name is Duke and Mr Basie's first name is 'Count'. The difference is that whereas I very much doubt that Mr Ellington ever tries to pass himself off as a duke, or Mr Basie ever pretends that he is a count, Mr Chilcottt makes every effort possible to pass himself off as a Lord. When he rings a restaurant to book a table, or a hotel to reserve a room, he tells the receptionist that his name is Lord Chilcott and always succeeds in making it sound as though the Lord were a genuine title, rather than simply a name. When he first telephoned the surgery, expecting to be able to make an appointment, Miss Johnson was very impressed and came running into my surgery to ask if we should give him an appointment before the surgery started. I told her that we do not have an appointments system and that we will never have an appointments system and that even if Her Majesty the Queen calls in for a consultation she will have to sit in the waiting room with the other patients and wait her turn. Miss Johnson was not impressed by this.

Mr Chilcott makes a real effort to look and sound very patrician. He wears his white hair long, combed straight back and curling over the collar, he always fastens his shirt cuffs with what look like heavy gold cufflinks and even in summer he always wear a three piece suit, with a gold chain across one side of his waistcoat, as though attached to a fob watch in the pocket.

'I get tired if I walk more than five or six miles,' he said, sitting down on the edge of my bed and giving me a jolt which made me wince. He didn't notice my wincing. 'And I get especially tired if I have to walk up steep hills.'

'Ah,' I said, not immediately being able to think of anything else more appropriate to say.

'I used to be able to walk to Barnstaple and back,' he said, rather defiantly.

'How old are you?' I asked.

'I'll be 92 next month,' he replied instantly, with considerable pride.

'I'm afraid I think you perhaps just have to come to terms with the fact that you're not as young as you were,' I told him, in too much pain to think of a more tactful way to break the news to him.

'Do you think that's it?' he asked, genuinely surprised.

'I'm afraid so.'

'The old ageing process catching up with me?'

'Yes.'

'Well I never,' he said. He stood up. 'So, what do you suggest?' he asked.

'Take shorter walks,' I said. 'Or just stop for a while and admire the view every so often.'

He thought for a while then nodded. 'Good advice, doctor,' he said. 'Would you syringe my ears while I'm here? I think the wax is building up again.'

I looked at him, hardly able to believe my own ears. I was lying flat on my back. It hurt to move. Most of my patients are thoughtful and appreciative. Lord Chilcott, as he always refers to himself, is one of those patients every doctor would happily manage without. He always sends me a cheap bottle of sherry at Christmas and for this he expects to be treated as a private patient. I would be far happier if he kept the sherry (which we never drink) and behaved a little more thoughtfully when visiting the surgery.

'If you pop along to the hospital, the nurse will syringe them for you,' I told him.

'But you usually syringe them yourself!' protested Mr Chilcott.

He was right, of course. I like to perform small procedures like syringing ears, removing stitches and sewing up small lacerations. I think it helps to cement the doctor-patient relationship if the doctor actually does something active from time to time.

'I would syringe your ears if I could,' I promised. 'And I will syringe your ears next time they're blocked. But I'm afraid I don't think I'll be able to syringe your ears from this position. You'll have to go the Brownlow Country Hotel this time.'

'Can't you sit up?'

I told him that I could not.

'Oh,' he said, 'I thought you were just perhaps having a bit of a lie in.'

'You'll have to go to the Brownlow Country Hotel,' I told him. I didn't have the energy or the patience to explain that I was not in bed out of choice.

Mr Chilcott looked puzzled. 'The hotel? I didn't know we had a hotel in Bilbury.'

'It's really the Bilbury hospital,' I explained. 'But we aren't allowed to call it a hospital.'

'Oh no, of course not,' agreed Mr Chilcott. 'Bloody silly if you ask me.'

He stood up and left without another word.

The fifth patient was Mrs Germander Speedwell who is in her 80s and in pretty good health for her age. Her biggest problem is that she is very aware of her age and expects to find every day a physical trial. She took one look at our stairs and said she didn't think she could manage them. So, since she was stuck downstairs and I was stuck upstairs, she stood in the hall and shouted up her replies to the questions I shouted down.

She wanted to know if I believed in euthanasia and said she was worried that when her time came she might not be able to deal very well with any accompanying pain. I promised her that I would make sure that she did not suffer any pain and Patsy said that she went away much happier than she'd been when she arrived.

During the day, word got round the village that the doctor had a bad back and was stuck in bed and the evening surgery was much quieter. Most people who might have come along decided that they could wait a day or so until I was able to see them in my consulting room, and examine them properly.

One patient did, however, turn up in the middle of the afternoon. It turned out to be someone I knew.

When I first met him, Jonquil Barley was working as a television presenter on an afternoon television chat show. (Astonishingly, he really did have a sister called Pearl. I think his parents had a sense of humour.) This was back in the days when I used to make regular television appearances. He was one of those energetic, excitable television people who always seem to be driven by clockwork and to have been wound up by an over-enthusiastic child. He had television hair (especially coiffed and gelled so that even in a hurricane not one hair would move a tenth of an inch), a television smile (permanently present and designed to show off his immaculately capped and whitened teeth) and a wardrobe full of beautifully fitting television suits.

Sadly, time did not treat him well.

He lost his hair and tried to deal with the loss by purchasing a toupee. The problem was that the viewers who had watched him balding were a little surprised to see him suddenly appear with a luxurious head of hair. Most television presenters deal with their hair loss gradually, as the loss occurs. Jonquil left it too late.

Worse still, when he had plastic surgery done to disguise the ravages of age, he went to a cut price surgeon who promised much but delivered little. And he went from having huge eyebags and a sagging chin to having skin so taut that it could have been used on a drum. Once again the viewers thought this hugely comical.

With no one taking him seriously as a television presenter, Jonquil, moved to radio where the hair and the skin were of no account. His agent found him a job presenting a local radio programme.

For a while all went well but Jonquil simply couldn't cope with the new life. He'd been accustomed to being a 'star', to having fans stop him in the street and ask for his autograph and to having production staff fussing around attending to his make-up, making sure that his suit jacket wasn't wrinkled and telling him how wonderful he was. He found working on the wireless something of an anti-climax and he started to drink more and more alcohol. On several occasions, he turned up late for work and once or twice listeners complained that he sounded drunk on the radio. Soon the boss of the radio station had to give him an official warning.

Jonquil then walked out of the radio station, telling everyone that he had been offered a fantastic job on a television station in

America. He organised a big party, which he could ill afford, and told big lies to everyone present. Colleagues and friends all wished him good luck.

I learned all this from him a year or two later.

He had found out where I was living and working and came to see me. He wanted to know if I could find him work. I rang round half a dozen people I knew at radio stations in the South West of England and eventually managed to get him a late night show on one of the stations.

The job lasted six weeks.

Jonquil was fired because he missed two programmes and was caught drinking alcohol while on the air.

That was, I think, the last paid employment he ever had.

He now looked awful. His face was flabby and he was fat. He was almost unrecognisable. His clothes were filthy and he smelt as if he hadn't bathed for a week or more. His nose and cheeks were red with the flush of a chronic alcoholic and he reeked of tobacco and booze.

He told me that he had been living rough in Exeter and remembering that I was in North Devon had hitchhiked his way up to Bilbury. It had taken him nearly two days.

'What can I do for you?' I asked him. I had no intention of trying to get him another job. I knew he'd let everyone down.

'Life's gone downhill a bit since I saw you last,' he said. It was the understatement of the century as far as I was concerned.

I told him I was sorry to hear it.

'Never could tell the difference between a dragon and a windmill,' he said, with a hollow laugh.

I smiled and nodded.

'I need a prescription,' he told me baldly. He explained that he wanted amphetamines and benzodiazepines.

'Can't live without the damned things,' he said. 'I'm weaning myself off them but it's a slow process as you know.'

I refused him.

'I'll give you the names of two clinics,' I told him. 'If you go there, and you're honest, they will help you.'

He swore and told me he didn't want to go to any bloody clinic. 'I've travelled for two days to come and see you,' he said angrily. He pulled his lips back in a strange sort of snarl. To someone lying in bed he actually looked quite frightening. 'I should have known better than to put my faith in some hick country doctor.'

'I'll give you some money to tide you over for a few days,' I told him. I made a supreme effort and reached for my wallet on the bedside table. It contained £60. It was all the cash we had in the house; a lot of money for us. I handed him the £30 which he took without a word. He then turned on his heel and walked out. When he had left, I realised that he hadn't once asked me why I was in bed in the middle of the day. I strongly suspected that the £30 would be blown on the drugs I'd refused to prescribe for him. He would doubtless know where to find what he needed.

'You haven't been sniffing laughing gas, have you?' asked Patsy, when she came upstairs to tell me that there were no more patients waiting to be seen. 'Mrs Rutter came downstairs as giggly as a schoolgirl and had her dress tucked into the back of her knickers and Tiggy Marwood came down saying something about you having a special offer on hernias.

'It's been a long morning,' I said with a sigh. I told her about Jonquil and our £60. 'And Lord Chilcott wanted me to syringe his ears while I lay flat on my back in bed.'

'At least he didn't come downstairs with his shirt hanging out of the back of his trousers,' said Patsy with a laugh.

I spent the rest of the afternoon lying in bed, trying to remember when Jonquil's life had begun to slide downhill. I eventually decided that he had probably always been doomed. I could remember a lot of small signs which should have told me which way things were going to go. It was all so, so sad.

There were just three patients at the evening surgery.

Mrs Mallory Spark, a divorcee in her thirties, had a recurrence of her cystitis. I scribbled out a prescription for an antibiotic though she has frequently told me that she suspects that her cystitis is usually a result of over energetic sexual activity with an exceptionally well endowed lover, rather than an infection. I have, however, found that if I don't prescribe an antibiotic her symptoms don't go away and I suspect that the story of the over demanding over endowed lover may well be more wishful thinking than rude reality.

Mr Albert Butt (known to everyone as 'Scuttle') came along complaining that his itchy feet were keeping him awake. With the aid of my shaving mirror and the mirror on Patsy's dressing table, I was able to examine his feet and make a diagnosis of athlete's foot. I prescribed some antifungal cream and promised him a good night's sleep.

The third patient, Norbert Hicklebury, complained that he thought he was going blind. He said he was frightened that he had macular degeneration – the disorder which had destroyed his father's quality of life. I was able to tell him that he had a cataract and that I would make an appointment for him to see an eye specialist. When I told him that the cataract could be treated, and that he would not lose his sight, he was almost deliriously happy.

After the end of the surgery, Patsy told me that she had noticed that a small bronze statue that had been standing on a table in the hall was missing. It was a statue of Napoleon on horseback; a rather nice three dimensional copy of the famous painting of Napoleon Bonaparte by the French artist Jacques-Louis David. Our good friends the Foggs, Patchy and Adrienne, had given it to us the previous Christmas.

'I think someone has stolen it,' she said sadly.

I knew who it was.

I don't know whether I was sadder at the disappearance of the bronze or at the fact that Jonquil had stolen it.

The rest of the evening was quiet. The telephone didn't ring once.

And the following day was quiet, too. There were just four patients at the morning surgery and two patients at the evening surgery. Two of the morning patients merely wanted repeat prescriptions. One wanted to know if I would be well enough to make her bottle of bitter green medicine when she ran out at the weekend (it contains nothing powerful and is my most popular and most effective placebo). I assured her that I would.

Three of the day's patients had come merely to bring me presents (one brought some old magazines, one brought a bottle of home-made whisky (I'm not sure whether or not it is as illegal to accept home-made whisky as it is to make it but I'm not going to say anything to the authorities and neither is the patient who made it) and the third brought a home embroidered card and a bunch of mixed flowers. Patsy allowed these three up into the bedroom (now turned into a temporary consulting room) and later told me that I had received more than a dozen 'Get Well' cards. She said that ten of the cards were identical and had clearly all been bought from Peter Marshall's shop.

And, praise the heavens, there were no urgent calls; no real emergencies which I could not deal with. The nearest thing to an emergency was the moment when Mrs Ossbury was stung by a bee. Mrs Ossbury is allergic to bee stings and has, in the past, suffered nasty reactions. Her husband brought her to the house for treatment and, understandably, they were both in quite a state. With Patsy's help, directing me and guiding my hand, I managed to give Mrs Ossbury an injection of adrenalin and the crisis was immediately averted. Mrs Ossbury left, I'm pleased to report, with the back of her skirt outside her knickers, which were nowhere near as voluminous as those worn by Mrs Rutter and had the words 'Welcome. Please Enter' embroidered on the front. She seemed very embarrassed when this was revealed and I got the distinct impression that she had not expected to visit the doctor when she'd got dressed earlier that day. Still, it could have been worse. I once saw a patient who wore panties with the words 'Tradesmen please use the back entrance' embroidered on them.

After two days in bed, fretting and doubtless increasingly irritable, I awoke on the third day and realised, with great delight, that the pain which had immobilised me was considerably better. Gingerly, I managed to slide out of bed and stand on my own two feet again. My sympathy for patients who need to spend long periods immobile was, as it is always is whenever I have to spend time in bed, massively enhanced. There is nothing like a little illness of their own to teach doctors to be more sympathetic when dealing with their patients.

I remembered that a medical school tutor of mine once said that all medical students should be forced to spend a week in bed every six months. That way, he said, they would never forget just how tiresome and exhausting it can be to be ill.

Granny Kennett's Pudding Club

A few months before Frank had his stroke, Frank and Gilly at the Duck and Puddle public house decided that they wanted to do a little 'pro-active marketing'.

It was actually Gilly, (who had obtained the phrase 'pro-active marketing' from a management magazine which a tourist left in the bar) who made the decision. Frank readily admits that if things were left to him there would be customs posts on every lane leading into the village and the pub would ban all outsiders. Thumper once claimed that Frank only became a licensee so that he could live in a pub and never run short of alcohol and Frank, who was there at the time, laughed, went an even deeper shade of red than is usual and agreed with him.

A group of us were sitting in the snug one lunch-time, when Gilly made her announcement. Thumper and Anne, Patchy and Adrienne were there, along with Peter Marshall and Patsy. It's rare to see Peter Marshall away from his shop during the daytime but Peter had closed for the morning because he'd been driving the hearse for the local undertaker. On his way home, he'd called in at the Duck and Puddle for half a shandy and a cheese sandwich. (Peter, a hard-working entrepreneur of the old school, has a number of jobs and would take on more responsibilities if he could persuade someone in authority to extend the number of hours in the day.)

'We need to do something to attract more visitors to the village,' Gilly said, to almost universal dismay and not a little astonishment. 'Every evening we see the same old faces in here and although we love you all dearly we need to persuade new customers to come into the pub.'

'Things are fine as they are,' protested Patchy, who regards anything new as an affront and has an oft-aired theory that all change must inevitably make things worse.

Frank, who obviously wasn't thinking straight, for if he had been he wouldn't have been so daft as to disagree with his wife, agreed with Patchy.

Gilly threw a beermat at Frank and told him to shut up.

Frank shut up.

The only person in the snug who thought that Gilly was talking sense was Peter Marshall.

Peter is always keen to persuade more people to come to the village. Since he has the only retail establishment for miles around he believes, not unreasonably, that if more visitors pass through the village then at least some of the money in the travellers' pockets will not go with them when they leave but will remain behind in his till.

Although he has no formal training in marketing, Peter, whose long established slogan is 'Buy One and Get What You Pay For', is forever coming up with new wheezes which will, he believes, turn his establishment into the heart of an international conglomerate. His long-term business plan is to float his shop on the stock market and sell shares to eager hedge fund operatives. Not long ago, he cleared out a shed next to his shop and he now rents this out to several local entrepreneurs, including a vet and a hairdresser. A few years ago he had a huge sign made which announced 'Buy One –Buy Another At The Same Price!' and could not understand why it didn't bring charabancs full of tourists flooding in from hotels in Lynton, Lynmouth and Ilfracombe. When one customer cheekily asked Peter for a discount, telling him that she thought he ought to take something off two shirts she was thinking of buying, Peter flew into a rage. He tore a sleeve off each of the shirts and asked her if that satisfied her.

Peter is always trying out new ways to ingratiate himself with potential customers and it is impossible not to admire his determination. A week ago, I went into his shop and found myself listening, in astonishment, as he told me detailed stories about his childhood. At the same time, I was encouraged to gaze in bewilderment as he showed me pictures of obscure relatives he claimed to have discovered in Northumberland and a particularly snowy and photogenic part of Canada. One of his relatives, he insisted, had a child with asthma. Several of his alleged relatives were beautiful young women whose photographs looked to me as though they had been clipped out of a magazine. When I eventually managed to stop the flow of information long enough to ask him what the devil he was doing, he explained that he had read in a book that a salesman should try to charm his customers, and ingratiate himself with them by sharing information about his own life and family. Since Peter doesn't have much of a life, and certainly doesn't have any family, I thought he was making a pretty good attempt to follow the author's advice. 'I wouldn't bother,' I told him, 'I only came in for a box of paperclips. And I'm going to buy those whether or not you show me pictures of people having a good time in the snowy wastes of Canada.' Peter sighed and tossed the pictures into a corner. I don't think he tried it on anyone else.

'We need to think of some way to persuade discerning people with taste and money to come to Bilbury,' said Gilly.

'I think it's a splendid idea,' said Peter, 'though I'm not sure we necessarily need discerning people with taste. I'd happily settle for people with money. And we have to be more business-like about the way we run the village. Just the other day, I had some people in the shop who had never even heard of Bilbury until they got here. They only found the village by mistake and once they'd got here they didn't know where they were because someone, whom I will not name, took down all the signposts.' He looked sternly at Thumper when he said this.

'Taking down the signs was necessary,' said Thumper, rather defensively. 'We had all that trouble with people thinking that the water in Bilbury would cure all their illnesses. We were knee deep in tourists and the lanes were clogged.'

The rest of us nodded our approval. The council had been a little upset about the disappearing road signs but since they refused to have any new ones made and couldn't find the old ones (they're hidden at the bottom of a silage silo on a farm in the village and not even the owner of the silo knows they are there).

'I always thought that was a missed opportunity,' grumbled Peter, who still sells bottled Bilbury water through the mail. He fills the bottles with water out of the tap and charges a small fortune for the stuff. It is rumoured that there is a man in Dubai who won't drink anything else and a man who works in the sorting office in Barnstaple once told me that Peter sends a crate of the stuff to Dubai every week. 'We could have handled that better,' continued Peter. 'We should have taken proper advantage of the situation.'

'That's as may be,' said Gilly, 'the water business was probably a bit too much of a good thing. I want to find something that will bring well-off, high-spending visitors to the pub. We don't need a lot of them and we don't need them here every day. We just need them and their money once a week or once a month.'

Peter, who had clearly already envisaged charabancs full of tourists arriving in the village on a daily basis, was obviously disappointed. The rest of us were relieved.

'You need something that brings in people from all over the country,' said Adrienne.

'But not too many of them,' said Thumper quickly.

'We could hold a second hand book fair,' suggested Adrienne. 'We could have stalls selling old books,' she looked around brightly, 'lots of people buy books so lots of people would come to Bilbury.'

'Great idea but a guy called Richard Booth has started something like that in Hay-on-Wye,' said Patchy. 'We need something original and exciting.'

'Oh,' said Adrienne. She seemed disappointed.

'But we don't want anything too exciting,' said Thumper. 'We don't want to fill the place with people.'

'You could offer cut price drinks,' said Peter Marshall. 'Half price beer for example. That would be very popular.'

'We'd lose money on every pint we sold,' said Gilly.

'In the retail trade it's called offering a loss leader,' said Peter.

I remembered, but tactfully didn't mention, that the only time Peter had offered a loss leader had been a disaster. It was, I remembered, a year or two ago, before the British currency was decimalised, and Peter had bought a small advertisement in the Barnstaple paper offering packets of biscuits for sixpence to customers who spent £1 on other groceries. There was subsequently some disquiet among customers, particularly the ones who had travelled from Barnstaple and Bideford, when they discovered that the packets of biscuits he was selling for sixpence contained just two ginger biscuits and had originally been packaged to be given away free on aeroplanes. Customers were even more upset when they discovered that the biscuits, which were in packages made for an airline called Air Enterprises which had gone bust in 1955, were all stale.

'I thought the idea was to think of something to bring people with money into the pub,' said Frank who had obviously been upset by the prospect of selling beer at half price.

'Of course it is,' said Gilly.

'How about a beer festival?' suggested Patchy. 'You could put tents up in the car park and have barrels of different types of real ale on sale.'

'Maybe just one tent,' said Thumper, who was obviously keen that the event, whatever it was, shouldn't bring too many people into the village.

'Oh, I don't think so,' said Gilly, pulling a face. 'Not a beer festival! There would be a lot of drunken people being sick in the flowerbeds.'

Frank, who had looked excited, now looked disappointed.

'Have you noticed how life is all about making decisions?' said Thumper, who had clearly been looking forward to a quiet hour in the pub. He paused and inspected a pork scratching before popping it into his mouth. 'Come to think about it, I suppose that not making a decision still means making a decision not to do something.'

'How about a gin festival?' suggested Patchy. 'Bit more up-market than a beer festival, don't you think?'

'People who are sick after drinking too much gin are just as likely to be sick as people who drink too much beer,' said Thumper. 'They only difference is that they always vomit in the lavatories.'

Gilly did not look as if she had been reassured by this.

'A whisky festival would be nice,' said Frank. 'Just a small festival with malt whisky tasting sessions. I could give lectures on the different types of malt whisky.'

'You'll drink any profits,' said Gilly firmly.

'You could have a dining club,' suggested Patsy. 'Once a week or once a month you could have a special dinner. People would join a club and have a slap up meal with a theme.'

'What sort of special dinner?' asked Frank, looking a little alarmed. 'What sort of 'theme'?'

'Once a month would probably be best,' said Thumper quickly. 'Don't want to make too much work for yourself do you?'

'Oh, I don't know what sort of theme,' said Patsy, replying to Frank. 'But I suppose you could have French food one week, Indian food another week, Thai food another week – something different every week.'

'Or once a month,' said Thumper.

'Or once a month,' agreed Patsy. 'You could call it a dinner club.'

'It's a wonderful idea but who could possibly cook all those different dishes?' asked Gilly, looking concerned. 'If we had to bring in a chef we'd probably end up spending more money than we were making.'

'Not the idea at all,' said Frank.

'Chip suppers once a month?' suggested Patchy. 'Simple enough.'

'We do those already,' Gilly reminded him. 'Ham and chips, egg and chips, sausage and chips. That's our menu.'

'And any variation on the theme,' said Frank. 'You can have ham, sausage, egg and chips if you like.'

'Probably best to forget about the whole thing,' said Thumper firmly. 'Never mind, we all tried.' He stood up. 'Time for another round everyone? I'm buying.'

'Splendid idea,' said Peter Marshall instantly. 'I'll have a whisky. Double please.' He finished the half a shandy he'd been drinking.'

'Very decent of you,' said Frank. 'I'll have a pint myself.' He stood up and walked over to the bar to start preparing the drinks. Discussions about how the Duck and Puddle could improve its cash flow situation were shelved while we all gave him our orders.

'What about just doing puddings?' suggested Patsy, when the new round of drinks had been distributed and Thumper had forked over the cash.

We all looked at her. She sipped her tomato juice.

'You could call it a pudding club!' she said brightly.

'What's a pudding club?' asked Frank.

'It's for women who are pregnant,' said Adrienne. She turned to her sister. 'Are you suggesting that we organise sex parties at the Duck and Puddle?'

I looked at Patsy and raised an eyebrow.

'Not that sort of pudding club!' said Patsy, blushing slightly. She looked at Adrienne. 'Trust you to think of that sort of pudding club!'

'Well what other sort of pudding club is there?' asked Adrienne.

'A dining club but you only serve puddings!' said Patsy.

I looked at her admiringly. I rather like puddings myself. I'm not so keen on broccoli and cabbage but I'm a devil for spotted dick and treacle pudding.

'What a brilliant idea!' said Gilly. 'Why hasn't anyone else thought of that?'

'Probably because my wife is brighter than everyone else!' I said, proudly.

'There was some sort of pudding club in America,' said Patchy, who has a vast reservoir of pretty well useless knowledge. 'I think it was at Harvard. But they only served the one pudding – something called Hasty Pudding.'

'What on earth is Hasty Pudding?' asked Frank. 'Something you knock up in a couple of minutes?'

'Probably,' laughed Patchy. 'I seem to remember it consisted of grains or corn cooked in milk or water. Doesn't sound all that much fun. A mushy sort of pudding. I think it's mentioned in the song 'Yankee Doodle'.'

'I can't see many people coming along to eat corn cooked in water,' said Frank, who doesn't really take to any food that doesn't contain at least 500 calories a portion. He shuddered at the thought.

'No, no, that's not the idea at all,' said Patsy. 'You offer people half a dozen different, traditional puddings – the sort of old-fashioned puddings that no one much bothers with any more. The sort of puddings that were served in schools.'

'Treacle pudding, roly poly pudding, spotted dick, bread pudding – that sort of thing!' I said, my mouth watering at the thought.

'You serve just puddings,' said Patsy, now warming to her theme. 'And people come along and pay a fixed price and can eat as many helpings of pudding as they want.'

'Those are all easy to make,' said Gilly.

'And cheap,' added Frank.

'It's not going to bring many people into Bilbury,' protested Peter who can be relied upon to think only of his own bottom line. 'And if you have the pudding club in the evenings how many of them are going to call in at my shop?'

'You can have the indigestion concession,' said Frank. 'Treacle pudding always gives me indigestion. You can supply us with a pile of different antacids which we'll put on a table by the door so that people can buy what they need as they're leaving.'

'I think this is a brilliant idea,' said Patchy. 'I love puddings. But those rich, stodgy puddings always give me terrible indigestion too.' He paused. 'But I don't care. I still eat them.'

'He does,' agreed Adrienne, who was still getting used to being a wife and running her own kitchen. 'I have to make three steamed puddings a week or else he sulks.'

'I'd need some help,' said Gilly. 'I'm not terribly good at puddings.'

'Granny Kennett!' said Patsy and I simultaneously.

The woman known as Granny Kennett is the grandmother of Patsy and Adrienne. Technically, since Patsy and I now have small children of our own, Patsy's mum should be known as 'Granny Kennett' but then the original 'Granny Kennett' would have to be 'Great Granny Kennett' and apart from being a bit of mouthful it would make everyone concerned feel very old. So Granny Kennett remains Granny Kennett.

Frank, Thumper and Patchy looked at me. Adrienne, Anne and Gilly looked at Patsy. Peter, who was busy working out what he could charge for bottles of indigestion medicine sold to a captive audience, didn't look up from the beermat upon which he was doing his calculations. Since he sells pens and pencils but never carries one himself, Peter was using a pen he'd borrowed from me. I watched him with some dismay since a pen which has been used to write on a beermat never again works properly.

'Granny Kennett makes the most marvellous puddings in the world!' cried Adrienne. 'What a brilliant idea!'

'We could call it Granny Kennett's Pudding Club!' said Gilly.

'Marvellous!' said Adrienne.

'Do you think she'd mind?' asked Gilly.

'She'd be as pleased as Punch!' said Patsy.

'She'd absolutely love it,' said Adrienne at the same time.

And so it was decided that the Duck and Puddle would introduce a new monthly Pudding Club, where diners would be invited to consume as many helpings of pudding as they could eat. All the puddings would be of the old-fashioned variety, served with a choice of either custard or custard, in other words no choice at all. Everyone agreed with Thumper that it would be best to hold the new Pudding Club monthly. Frank said that he would put up a poster and insert a small and inexpensive advertisement in the Barnstaple newspaper.

Peter Marshall said that if Frank made two posters he would stick one up in his shop since he had been given the antacid concession.

When, later in the day, Patsy and Adrienne went round to see her, Granny Kennett was, as her granddaughters had predicted, absolutely delighted that the Pudding Club was being named after her and she readily agreed to join Gilly in preparing the puddings.

During the three weeks which followed, much time was spent selecting the puddings for the inaugural meeting of the Club and the recipes were carefully honed and polished. (Editor's Note: the recipes appear at the back of this book under the imaginative heading of 'Granny Kennett's Pudding Club Recipes'.)

To everyone's absolute delight, the Granny Kennett Pudding Club proved enormously successful. And, more to the point perhaps, it actually proved rather profitable for Frank and Gilly.

Granny Kennett steadfastly refused to take any payment for her services or for her recipes (she was, she said and meant, absolutely thrilled to be part of such an exciting culinary venture) and Peter Marshall, usually so very careful to watch every penny, was persuaded to hand over a small portion of his profits from the sale of indigestion remedies to the Duck and Puddle 'Let's Actually Make a Profit For Once Fund'.

The first customers were, inevitably, the locals and the citizens of Bilbury turned out in some force to join the Pudding Club. The whole venture was so successful that Gilly predicted that before long there would be Pudding Clubs at pubs, restaurants and hotels all over England. Patsy's idea had, it seemed, proved extremely attractive to customers of a certain age. Without exception, the customers who joined the Club were over the age of 40. All could remember stodgy, steamed puddings from their childhoods. All wanted to recapture the joy of a treacle sponge and the filling delight of a rich, well-made plum pudding covered in a thick custard. (Gilly decided right from the start that it would be impossible to have a Pudding Club without having a plum pudding on the menu. Granny Kennett concurred, saying that when she had been a girl her mother had made plum pudding several times throughout the year. It had not, she said, been exclusively reserved for Christmas.)

Outsiders only started to attend the Pudding Club evenings after the third week. And that was when, from my point of view, the trouble really started.

The people who live in Bilbury tend to have large appetites. Most of them lead arduous lives and can burn up a good number of calories in an ordinary day. Even so, most were sensible enough to know when to stop.

However, something designed as an integral part of the attraction turned out to be a bit of a problem.

One of the basic principles of the Granny Kennett Pudding Club was that members would pay a membership fee to join the club, and a fee for each meeting of the club which they attended, but they would not pay separately for each pudding they ate. At least six different puddings would be served during an evening and all the members present were entitled to enjoy as many of the puddings as they thought they could manage. Moreover, members were perfectly entitled to request second, third, fourth or more helpings. There were, as Frank put it, 'no limits'.

(Nothing happened at these club meetings, except that a number of fine puddings were served. There were no minutes and no agenda, but it seemed rather fun to describe the culinary entertainments as 'meetings' for it enabled everyone attending to say, if faced with an invitation or commitment which they wanted to avoid, that they had to attend a 'meeting' in the village. This excuse quickly became as popular with villagers as is the excuse 'I have to go on a course' is with golfers.)

The problem with allowing people to eat unlimited amounts of food is that some of them will try to do just that.

And that is when the problems started.

When people have driven thirty miles to eat steamed puddings they arrive determined to get their money's worth. They want to eat everything available, and they want to eat it all two or three times. People turned out to be even greedier when they had booked themselves into a room at the Duck and Puddle. It turns out that if you've driven thirty miles and booked a hotel room for the night then you want to eat everything available at least five or six times. And hang the consequences.

Things got so bad that I began to dread the monthly meeting of the Granny Kennett Pudding Club. I knew that at the end of the evening, and sometimes before the end of the evening, I would find myself ministering unto the sick, the very sick and the exceedingly unfortunate few who were convinced that they were dying. After a few months of this I gave up attending the pudding club myself and simply sat in the snug, quietly nursing something suitable and waiting for my services to be required.

Very few of those who over-ate seemed to regard their condition as being in any way related to their inability to know when to say: 'No, thank you. That was delicious but I couldn't eat another morsel'. Some blamed Granny Kennett, some blamed Gilly and some (for reasons which I never began to understand) blamed me.

And, although none of us had predicted this, for in Bilbury we are not a litigious lot, the evening came when one unhappy customer announced that he intended to take legal action against Gilly, Frank and the Duck and Puddle.

'Your puddings made me ill,' he complained, announcing to Gilly that she and her husband and everyone else involved would be hearing from his solicitors.

It did absolutely no good at all for Gilly to point out that he had eaten four helpings of Spotted Dick, three helpings of Treacle Sponge, three helpings of Plum Pudding and two helpings each of every other pudding on the menu. And that he had done all this entirely of his own volition. No one had held him down and forced puddings down his throat.

The man was adamant. He felt bloated, sated, full and about to die and, if he lived, he would sue. And he said that the fact that I was sitting in the snug, ready to offer professional succour to the greedy and the over-enthusiastic, proved that the damage done to his intestines was predetermined and premeditated and done with malice aforethought. He said that I was clearly a 'pudding chaser' and that I was hanging around in the pub with the express intention of making money out of his distress. Even when I pointed out that I had not charged him for my services, or for the medication I had prescribed (and had not charged anyone else) he remained adamant that I would be hearing from his solicitors.

In the end, Gilly and Frank had to pay several hundred pounds to prevent the case going to court.

The costs of the legal action, and the damages they were advised to pay, wiped out all the profit they had made. I managed to get away with an abject apology.

After that experience, Gilly decided that she would stop promoting the Granny Kennett Pudding Club outside the village. The posters in the Duck and Puddle and Peter Marshall's shop were removed and no more advertisements were placed in the local papers. Only locals were allowed to be members of the club.

And the little table which Peter Marshall set up for every meeting, and which contained a good selection of proprietary antacids, proved perfectly adequate for dealing with the inevitable digestive upsets which were, and still are, a consequence of dining at Granny Kennett's Pudding Club.

Patsy and I re-joined the club, and our monthly consumption of steamed and stodgy puddings is now the highlight of our limited social calendar.

However, there is no doubt that the puddings which are provided are sometimes a strain even for a healthy digestive system and although I like to think I know when to say 'No, thank you, that was splendid but I really couldn't eat another mouthful' I am not too proud to admit that even I have been known to take advantage of what has come to be known as 'Peter Marshall's Final Pudding Selection'.

These days the antacids do not rest on the hall table, but Frank brings them round on a tray, as though carrying around the cheese board.

I always choose something liquid (liquid medicines are considerably faster acting than antacid medicines in tablet form) and my personal preference is for a tablespoonful of something with a pleasant minty flavour.

I find it rounds off the evening very nicely.

Sir Chauncey's Oak Tree

On the edge of the Bilbury village green, not far from the church of St Crispin and St Ermentrude, stands an enormous oak; a tree which has been part of the Bilbury scenery for far longer than anyone alive can remember. The tree was split by lightning in the early 19th century and even back then the tree was old and was held in great esteem. Indeed, it was so much loved that it was repaired with a number of iron bands commissioned by Sir Chauncey Harvester, a local landowner. The iron bands were made and fastened into place by the local blacksmith, a huge man called Jack Turberry, who was said to be so strong that he could bend horseshoes with his bare hands. The repair of Sir Chauncey's Oak Tree was, quite possibly, the first example of tree surgery anywhere in the world and today barely a month goes by without a tree surgeon from somewhere on the planet visiting the site to make an inspection and take photographs.

There was a scare in 1964 when a gale removed several of the higher branches but the tree survived and recovered and today it looks set fair to last another few hundred years. It is important to the village because it is a tangible sign of our history.

Other villages in North Devon have legends and myths to give them a sense of identity. Witchcraft and sorcery are ripe in this part of the county and there are many local villages which have strange tales to tell and which are well populated with witches and ghosts.

There is, for example, the white witch of Culborough Down.

In the early 19th century, a Reverend Inkborough, was the local clergyman in Bampton Leys. The Reverend Inkborough was the second son of a very rich north country businessman who had made his money out of the cotton trade. There was an elder son, who would inherit the big house, the land and the factory, and so Mr Inkborough had bought the living for his younger son. You could do that in those days – buying a young son a post as a clergyman in the same way that you could buy yourself a seat in the House of Commons.

The son, may have been a clergyman but he was terribly mean and he built a roadside hut for his wife, Imelda, so that she could sell teas and snacks to visitors. This was, at the time, considered a very eccentric thing to do and business was at first slow.

Mrs Inkborough realised that what she was doing was considered rather odd and so she built on that, turning a disadvantage into a benefit, and began to tell tales of the Doones and other local legends. She also started dispensing medicines to travellers as well as villagers – basing the medicines she prepared on local myths. What had begun as Ye Olde Original Tea Shoppe soon became an early 19th century drugstore. Mrs Inkborough became quite famous. She soon became known as a local white witch, and was talked about as 'Mother Imelda' although she didn't have any children of her own. After she died many people claimed that they saw her by the roadside and as late as the 1920s three separate instances were recorded when tourists claim to have bought refreshments from her and one claimed to have bought a paste guaranteed to cure blistered feet.

Then there is the Withycombe witch, Joan Carne, who lived in the 16th century. Mrs Carne was said to have been a black witch who killed three husbands by casting bad spells on them. Despite this, which might have been seen as something of a flaw by some, she was well liked locally (especially by the people she didn't marry) and when she herself died her funeral attracted a huge number of people. When the mourners got back to her house after the service, expecting to make do with the usual simple meal of buns and ale, they found Joan's ghost preparing a meal of bacon and eggs. I'm pleased to say that they all tucked in and had a damned good wake.

Bilbury, I am relieved to say, just has the tree.

Tradition has it that the tree was important to Sir Chauncery, who did not have much of a local reputation for mending trees, because it was the site of his dalliance with a girl called Esmerelda; a young maiden who was the daughter of the local vicar.

The vicar had forbidden the match in view of the fact that Sir Chauncey (who was 54 years older than Esmerelda) had something of a reputation as a ladies' man. The reputation was not undeserved for Sir Chauncey is said to have worked his way through five wives and countless mistresses.

It is, perhaps, not entirely surprising that both the vicar and his good lady wife thought the match 'unsuitable' even though it would have meant their daughter marrying into the local aristocracy, becoming Lady Esmerelda and, before too long one assumes, the owner of a large house and over a thousand acres of prime Devon and Somerset farmland. How much these considerations influenced the young Esmerelda is not recorded though sceptics might assume that they were not entirely ignored when she was weighing up the competitive attractions of Sir Chauncery and any one of the local beaus who would, presumably, have paid court to such a nubile young woman but who would have doubtless expected their wives to live in far more modest circumstances.

(As an aside, and for the sake of completeness, I think it is worth mentioning that Sir Chauncey is not only famous for rescuing a sick tree but is also believed in Bilbury to be famous, or perhaps that should be infamous, as the Man of Porlock. In the summer of 1797, the poet Samuel Taylor Coleridge, who was feeling more than a little under the weather at the time, moved to the Quantock hills in nearby Somerset and took a cottage above the sea near to the village of Culbone. Coleridge, who was born in South Devon and was a romantic sort of fellow, suffered a good deal from stress and from a rheumatic illness and he rather hoped that the bracing sea air would ameliorate his symptoms. It has been pointed out that he and his friend Thomas de Quincy, the author of *The Confessions of an Opium Eater*, were enthusiastic users of laudanum and it is perfectly possible that both of them might have felt a little better if they had consumed a little less opium, but that's as maybe and making judgements about people's behaviour in bygone times is neither fair nor profitable. Anyway, the story has it that Coleridge fell asleep, or into a drugged stupor, while reading a book about Kubla Khan, the Mongol leader. When he awoke, a good while later, he had a poem about Kubla Khan fully formed in his head and he immediately started to scribble down the verses as he remembered them. We can probably all imagine his desperate attempt to write down the contents of his dream before they disappeared into that place that dreams go when our concentration is, for a moment, distracted and dreams are displaced by prosaic thoughts inspired by the present.

Sadly for him and for us, when Coleridge had written down 54 lines of his poem there was a knock on the door. Polite to a fault, Coleridge answered the knock only to find his landlord, Sir Chauncey standing there demanding that they go out together and inspect some aspect of the cottage which Sir Chauncey owned and which Coleridge was renting. This was probably a wobbly drainpipe or a chimney which needed pointing. Coleridge, painfully aware that the rest of his poem was disappearing by the second, had little choice but to obey. By the time Sir Chauncey, now known to the world as the 'Man of Porlock' or 'Person of Porlock' – now a widely used literary allusion to any unwelcome intruder who disrupts whatever one is doing – had tottered off, and the unfortunate Coleridge had forgotten the rest of the poem. And so the poem about Kubla Khan never got any further than the 54 lines Coleridge had written down before Sir Chauncey's untimely arrival.)

Bilbury's most illustrious tree, which is now known to everyone as Sir Chauncey's Oak Tree (but also known to locals simply as 'the tree'), has, over the years, produced its fair share of problems.

So, for example, small boys would, from time to time, try climbing it, and would then fall off and break a bone or two.

But apart from this, I never thought of the tree as presenting any sort of health hazard.

But I was wrong in that.

And although, like everyone else in Bilbury, I have great affection and respect for the tree, which is a symbol of the village's history and a huge connection with our past, there was a time when, just for a few hours, I would have happily seen the damned thing chopped down and turned into furniture and fire wood.

The worst crisis occasioned by Sir Chauncey's Tree did not involve a single small boy with a broken bone but a serious scare when a number of children in the village suddenly fell ill one autumn afternoon.

I was called to the village school because seven children were complaining of nausea and abdominal pain. By the time I got to the school, three of them had produced some fairly nasty looking, and bloody, diarrhoea. It's true that diarrhoea never looks very pleasant. But when it contains blood it looks especially scary.

Because so many of the children had been taken ill at the same time, it didn't need Sherlock Holmes or Dr John Watson to work out that the children must have eaten something which had upset them. And it didn't take much questioning before I found out what it was.

The children who were ill had all been eating acorns, collected in handfuls from underneath Sir Chauncey's Tree, the largest and most productive oak tree in the village. Every autumn the tree must produce several thousand of its famous seeds. Walk underneath St Chauncey's Tree and you can feel and hear the acorns crunching beneath your feet.

Acorns contain an enormous amount of tannic acid and are toxic if eaten in large quantities. Farmers always worry about them because acorns are poisonous to cattle, especially the young, and to horses. They can be deadly to dogs too. Since sheep can safely eat up to half a pound of acorns a day without coming to any harm, and adult pigs can eat double that, the farmers in Bilbury usually put sheep into a field to clear out the acorns before putting in cattle. Ducks and hens seem to eat acorns without any bad effects, though the acorns discolour the eggshells, but acorns and cattle definitely do not mix. My father-in-law, Mr Kennett always puts a couple of dozen sheep into fields where there are oak trees so that they will eat up the acorns before the cows are let in.

Unfortunately, of course, Sir Chauncey's Tree sits on the edge of the unfenced village green which isn't used for grazing. And so the acorns just lie around on the ground. No one bothers to collect them these days because you can't do much with a handful of acorns.

Back in the days before Peter Marshall sold several varieties of instant coffee, country folk used to roast acorns and make their own version of a type of coffee; a cheap drink which was said to be good for patients with tuberculosis and for delicate children.

The acorns were gathered when they were ripe, shelled, cut into pieces and dried before the fire, or in an oven. Some folk would leach the acorns to remove the intense bitterness – repeatedly boiling them in water until the water stopped turning brown and then cutting and drying them. Gypsies used to put a bag of ripe, brown acorns into a running stream and leave them there for a couple of days to remove the bitter taste. The dried acorns were then roasted like coffee beans, ground or pounded into a powder, mixed with a little melted butter and kept in airtight jars. The powder was then used like coffee with half an ounce of acorn powder to the pint of water for adults and around half that for children. Just as with ordinary coffee, sugar and milk could be added to taste. Some villagers and travelling folk mixed ground coffee with ground acorns.

The village children, had somehow heard of this and had collected a huge pile of green acorns, pounded them into a powder and made their own version of acorn coffee. But they had not done the job properly and they had not removed the tannic acid. They had also made the drink deadly strong and they had masked the bitterness by adding plenty of sugar. Some of the children had even chewed and swallowed whole acorns. How they managed this is beyond me. Afterwards, as a small experiment, I tried a taste of a small portion of acorn and I had to spit it out immediately. I think the children who ate the acorns whole were merely showing off to one another; each one trying to prove how tough he was. It is, I think, no coincidence that only boys had eaten the acorns whole. Girls had drunk the acorn coffee mixture but they hadn't chewed the raw acorns.

The children who had drunk the acorn mixture were in a terrible state when I saw them. They had awful diarrhoea but they were vomiting too and not surprisingly the poor school mistress didn't know what to do. I believe teachers are given some basic first aid training but no teacher could have been trained to prepare for this sort of disaster. Not surprisingly, the remaining children, the ones who were still healthy, were beginning to cry and I could see we were heading for some pretty wild hysterics. The problem was that until I arrived, no one had worked out what had caused the diarrhoea and sickness and so the children who were still well and who had not consumed any acorns assumed that they were about to fall ill too.

The whole thing was something of a nightmare.

I immediately told the school teacher to separate out all the children who had eaten acorns from those who had not. The ones who had not were kept in the classroom and the ones who had were taken outside. There is only one classroom in the village school so there was really nowhere else to put them. I then told the teacher to telephone Bradshaw, my district nurse, and to ask him to come to the school as quickly as possible. I also told her to telephone as many of the parents of the affected children and, preferably without worrying them, to ask them to pop along to the school as quickly as they could. I needed the parents to comfort the children and I needed Bradshaw because I had to make all the children vomit up the acorns they'd swallowed. It seemed from questioning a few of the children that their acorn experiment had taken place no more than an hour earlier. If I sent the children to Barnstaple it would be at least another hour before we could them there. Most of the parents do not have motor cars and I couldn't get more than three sick children and a couple of parents in the Rolls. We needed to move quickly because the acorn mixture the children had taken is very poisonous to young bodies and would cause kidney and liver damage. I was genuinely worried that some of the children would die if we didn't act quickly.

There are several ways to make children vomit, but sticking two fingers down the back of a child's throat is as good a method as any and has the advantage of being quick as well as effective. So that was how Bradshaw and I spent our time that day.

That all happened a year or two ago and these days the local school teacher always gives the children a stern warning about the dangers of eating acorns or, indeed, any other seeds or fruits which they don't know for certain to be safe.

The most recent problem relating to Sir Chauncey's Oak Tree happened during the night.

I was woken by a hammering on the front door.

I pulled on a dressing gown, tottered downstairs and found Peter Marshall standing on the doorstep. It was, I remember thinking at the time, typical of Peter to walk around to the house rather than spend a couple of pennies making a telephone call.

Peter, who lives above his shop which overlooks the village green, told me that he had been awoken by great cries coming from the village green. He said that at first he thought it was aliens who had landed on the green and had got their spaceship tangled up with some of the tree branches (he had, he explained, been watching a programme about aliens and space ships a couple of nights earlier) but when he had woken properly he suspected it was young folk larking about. Looking out of his bedroom window he'd been unable to see any spaceships or gallivanting youths but had spotted someone writhing around on the grass and had realised that this was the source of the cries. There was a full moon that night and visibility, even at 3 o'clock in the morning, was pretty good.

'It's Mr Wallis,' said Peter, 'I've no idea what he's doing out there in the middle of the night.'

Max Wallis is something of a recluse but this is not because he is shy or lacks confidence. On the contrary, he has little to do with the village, or the villagers, because he considers himself to be very superior to us all. He does something financially rewarding in London (I gather it is something to do with 'financial services') and spends most of his time there, coming down to Bilbury only for occasional weekends. He and his wife, Deidre, usually bring with them several of their smart London friends. They are rarely seen around the village. They do not patronise Peter Marshall's shop and never visit the Duck and Puddle.

When I got to Mr Wallis, I found that he had a broken arm and a broken ankle. I gave him an injection for the pain and sent Peter off to telephone for an ambulance. He was happy to do that because a 999 call doesn't cost anything.

'What on earth happened?' I asked Mr Wallis. I then noticed that there was a ladder leaning up against the tree. 'Had you been climbing the tree?'

Looking rather embarrassed, Mr Wallis admitted, that he had indeed been up the tree.

'Why were you climbing the tree at this time of the morning?' I asked.

Mr Wallis wouldn't answer but when I looked around a little more I spotted a hammer and then I saw a bag of copper nails on the ground.

'You were trying to kill Sir Chauncey's Oak, weren't you?'

There is a myth that if you hammer copper nails into a tree you'll kill it. It's nonsense of course but people still believe the myth.

Mr Wallis has a large house on the edge of the village green. He has repeatedly demanded that the tree be felled because it interferes with his view over Bilbury and North Devon. He lost his battle to have the tree removed when the local council put a Tree Preservation Order on it and protected it for life from people with saws and axes.

Mr Wallis obviously didn't know this but he wasn't the first person in the village to try to kill that tree and he's not even the first to try to kill it with copper nails. Seventy or so years ago, a vandal who also thought the tree interfered with the view from his house hammered copper nails into the trunk in an attempt to kill it. The tree was unaffected, and if you look hard you can still see some of the nails. The vandal who tried to murder the tree died half a century ago but the tree flourishes still.

The ambulance eventually arrived and took Mr Wallis to the hospital to have his broken bones dealt with. When the ambulance had gone, Peter and I moved the ladder, the hammer and the nails and put them in the shed behind Mr Wallis's house. There were still no lights on the house and no signs of life. We had rung the doorbell in the hope that there might be someone interested in Mr Wallis's fate but although we had heard some scuffling and I'd spotted a curtain twitching no one had come to the door.

A week or so after this incident, I sat in the Duck and Puddle discussing the case of Sir Chauncey's Oak with Patchy. We both agreed that we needed to go round and have a word with Mr Wallis, to remind him that the tree was protected by law and warn him against trying to damage it again.

We were trying to decide whether it would be better for us to go together or for us to put together a deputation representing the village as a whole when Thumper Robinson wandered in.

We told him what we were discussing.

'Mr Wallis won't try to damage the tree again,' said Thumper, with quiet confidence.

'How do you know?' Patchy asked him. 'How can you be so sure?'

'I went round and told him that I like that tree,' said Thumper, who was clearly very angry that someone had tried to kill the old oak.

I now share Thumper's confidence that Sir Chauncey's Tree is safe. And there is no need for a deputation to remind Mr Wallis that the tree is out of bounds.

Thumper can be very convincing.

Carlton's Long Goodbye

England is falling into the sea. In some places it is falling into the sea quite slowly. In other places it is falling into the sea quite quickly. Long stretches of the coastline are at risk and the problem is particularly acute along the coast of south Devon and Dorset where the cliffs are made of chalk or sand which have a regrettable tendency to crumble and fall away as easily as if they were made of puff pastry. There are parts of the coast in South Devon and along the Dorset coast where house owners report having lost 10 to 20 feet of garden in a year. Many home owners who thought they were living in very desirable residences are now living in properties which are unsaleable and, in practical terms, entirely worthless.

As a general rule, it is usually difficult or impossible to lose all your money if you buy a house. Even if the house has dry rot, wet rot, termites and woodworm the building site will usually still have a notable value.

But if you are foolish enough to buy a house on the edge of a cliff, and the house and its underlying building plot subsequently fall into the sea, then all your money will be lost.

It is, perhaps, hardly surprising that there are now beautiful coastal properties on sale which have been valued at just £1 for the freehold. No one will buy them. No bank or mortgage company will lend money on them. No insurance company will insure them. Indeed, insurance companies won't even insure coastal properties against fire because they fear that owners may set fire to their own homes before they disappear with the cliff, into the sea. Solicitors and property experts in some parts of England now advise their clients that if you can hit a golf ball into the sea from the garden then you shouldn't even consider buying the house. England is shrinking at an extraordinary rate and thousands of home owners are now sitting waiting for their home to be declared uninhabitable. The authorities have effectively written off hundreds of miles of coastline, and all the small ports and villages which are situated in or along the coast. Many beauty spots will disappear. Coastal paths will soon exist only on old maps.

Most of the North Devon coast is rocky, and compared to the coastline of the southern part of the country, there is relatively little erosion. But there are exceptions, as there always are, of course, and there are houses on North Devon's cliff edge which are, year by year, inexorably moving closer to disaster.

In my book *Bilbury Tonic* I described how my patients Mrs Iolanthe Fielding and her considerably younger husband, Bertie live in an unsaleable house, with spectacular views, on the North Devon cliffs. The Fieldings pay just £5 a month in rent for a neat two bedroomed white-washed cottage with a decent sized garden and spectacular sea views. The rent is ridiculously low because, although the house had been on the market for three years, with an absurdly modest asking price of just £200, there have been no takers. One or two London buyers had shown interest, thinking that they had perhaps spotted the bargain of a lifetime, but when they saw that two neighbouring cottages had already fallen down onto the rocks below they quickly withdrew their offers and hot-footed it back to the big city where houses tend to stay where they've been built and, generally speaking, show very little inclination to wander.

Another of my patients, Carlton Tregallon, lives on the same stretch of coast.

Actually, to be accurate, Carlton lived in what used to be a garden shed sitting in the garden of a 17th century property. The house undoubtedly had wonderful sea views when it was built. The house has gone but the shed remains.

And I refer to him in the past tense because Carlton died not long ago.

I used to see Carlton around the village most weeks but I saw him in my professional capacity only once in my life; when he fell out of an apple tree and broke the ulna bone in his left forearm. It was Carlton's ulna bone but it was, inevitably, someone else's apple tree. He was in his late 60s at the time and probably the oldest scrumper in the country. I remember that I had a hell of a job to persuade him to go to the hospital in Barnstaple. In the end, I had to stick him in the car and take him over to the casualty department myself. I remember he told the young casualty doctor that he had tripped and fallen down the stairs. He was too embarrassed to admit that he had made a townsman's mistake and crawled out too far on a half rotten branch.

Carlton was something of a hermit. He worked as a part-time freelance shepherd but he was also a scrounger. He was a simple fellow who never wasted anything. When he ate an apple, he ate the core. He didn't own a needle or any thread and if his socks had holes in them he would wear them for as long as there was sock to show above the sides of his shoes.

He was married once, though it was a very brief arrangement. It happened before I arrived in Bilbury but Dr Brownlow told me all about it.

Carlton was a dyed in the wool countryman who hardly ever went anywhere which involved a journey that couldn't be made on foot, but back in the early 1960s, he went to a funeral in Birmingham. While he was in the city, he met a widow called Beryl with whom he established something of a rapport. She was slender, maidenly and entirely not the sort of woman one would have expected to become Carlton's life partner. He was breezy and carefree. She was careful and deliberate. He had an earthy sense of humour and a loud cackling laugh. She had thin lips which looked as if they had never entertained a smile or, heaven forbid, a kiss.

After Carlton's return to Bilbury, the two of them communicated for a while by telephone and letter and eventually, to the utter astonishment and quiet bewilderment of everyone who knew either of them, the pair decided that they were in love and that they should get married. It was, people thought, perhaps a case of opposites attracting.

So Carlton, accompanied by Thumper, Patchy and a couple of other pals, went up to Birmingham in Thumper's truck and after a good time had been had by all, Thumper, Patchy and the others returned to Bilbury while Carlton remained behind with his new bride. Beryl lived in a small, neat terraced house in a suburb of Birmingham called Handsworth and she was employed as a secretary by a firm of solicitors who had offices in the city centre. The newlyweds decided to spend their honeymoon in Handsworth.

'What is the point in going all the way to the Bahamas when you're going to spend all your time in bed?' asked Carlton.

And so they drew the curtains, stayed in bed and, it is to be hoped, both had a wonderful time.

Carlton insisted afterwards that he had genuinely believed that he would be able to live happily in Handsworth but those who know him well say that they always had serious doubts.

Everything went wonderfully well for two days, which was the amount of time which Beryl had taken off work for her honeymoon, but then, on the third morning, the Wednesday, Beryl arose at 7.30 a.m., had a quick breakfast and hurried out to catch a bus which would take her into the city centre in time to start work in the solicitors' office.

Carlton, who had no job to go to and, since his own work experience was entirely with sheep, very little prospect of finding anything for which he was even remotely suited, stayed behind in the terraced house in Handsworth. There are few, if any, sheep in Handsworth.

He mowed the tiny lawn, pruned the six rose bushes, had a cup of tea, mowed the lawn again, pruned the six rose bushes a little more and then sat in a chair in the kitchen and, looking at the clock, realised that it was still only ten past nine and that he had another nine hours to kill before Beryl would be back home.

Carlton then went for a walk, found a small park and sat on a bench until the public houses opened at 12 noon. He stayed in a pub called the Dog and Ferret until it shut at 2.40 p.m. and then, despite the fact that it was raining, went back to the park, lay down on park bench and went to sleep.

At 3.30 p.m., he was arrested for vagrancy.

Under the Vagrancy Act 1824 (the full title of which *An Act for the punishment of idle and disorderly persons, rogues and vagabonds*) it is an offence for anyone to sleep rough and anyone in England and Wales. Anyone who is found to be homeless or 'trying to cadge subsistence money' can be arrested.

Carlton, who still insisted on tying his ancient ragged overcoat with orange baler twine, protested that he was a solid and upright citizen and a married man to boot but the policeman, who was young and who had never seen a man with his coat tied together with string who wasn't a vagrant, was neither impressed nor convinced.

Beryl, with the help of one of the young solicitors at the offices where she worked, succeeded in extracting Carlton from the police station to which he had been taken and persuading the station sergeant that no charges should be brought. Carlton apologised profusely for kicking the policeman on the ankle and insisted that he had slipped on wet grass and lost his balance. Beryl, who had never been so embarrassed in her whole life, was allowed to leave work early in order to take her husband home.

It would, perhaps, have been better for all concerned if the two protagonists had decided there and then to call it a day, cut their losses, kiss each other goodbye and agree that a mistake had been made and that compatibility and good sense had been overruled by an attack of wholesome lust.

But Carlton somehow managed to persuade Beryl that they would have a future together if she would agree to move with him to Bilbury where he would be able to resume his work as a freelance shepherd, working for whichever local farmer required assistance. He told her that he was confident that she would be able to find suitable employment in an office in Barnstaple though no one, certainly not Carlton, could possibly say from whence this confidence was derived. He said that they would live in the small cottage he rented and, when the house in Handsworth had been sold, they would be able to buy a small home for themselves in Bilbury or one of the neighbouring villages.

And so Beryl rang her employer and said that she would not be returning to work and the pair of them packed a bag each, took the bus to the station and began the journey to Bilbury. Since they did not have a car and, in any case neither of them had a driving licence, this was a complicated business which involved taking a train to Bristol, another train to Exeter and a third train to Barnstaple. By the time they arrived in Barnstaple, the day's only bus had long since gone and so Carlton telephoned Thumper who collected the happy couple from the Barnstaple station and took them to Carlton's cottage.

It has to be said that Carlton undoubtedly erred in describing his shed as a cottage. Beryl, being a town girl, had envisaged a cottage rather along the lines of the sort of thing portrayed on the lids of chocolate boxes. She had expected a thatched roof, roses around the door and a garden filled with hollyhocks, foxgloves and honeysuckle. What she got, however, was a tumbledown shack with a corrugated iron roof, no indoor plumbing and no electricity. A decade earlier, the shack had been the garden shed in the garden of an extremely well built, pleasant house. But, thanks to bad weather and an eroding cliff, the house had been split into two parts. One half, now a ruin, stood on the very edge of the cliff. The remains of the other half of the property lay on the beach below. The owner had died and there were no relatives so the council had never been able to find anyone to take on the responsibility of clearing up the debris. The sea was steadily doing the work free of charge.

There were no utility services at Carlton's shack.

Drinking water was obtained from a couple of old oil drums, which collected rainwater via a complicated system involving an old sail and some plastic drainpipes. The toilet facilities consisted of a very primitive, cupboard-sized privy with no seat. This was positioned over a cesspit which was situated about twenty yards away from the shack.

This was not what Beryl had signed up for and whereas Carlton had lasted for three nights in Handsworth she did not last for one night in Bilbury.

Too angry for tears she demanded that Thumper take her back to the railway station in Barnstaple where, she insisted, she would wait for the first train back to civilisation. Thumper's suggestion that she and Carlton stay the night with him or at the Duck and Puddle did not meet with approval.

And that was the end of the marriage.

Carlton and Beryl never got divorced and so technically they were still married at the time of Carlton's demise but they hadn't seen or spoken to each other since Beryl fled back to Birmingham. Carlton had gone back to being a bachelor and Beryl had got her job back as a secretary for a legal firm.

They had both learned valuable lessons.

Carlton died of a massive heart attack while walking back home from the Duck and Puddle and was found the following morning by a farmer who saw his body on the roadside. He had a smile on his face and looked as serenely happy as anyone can expect to be when they are lying dead by the roadside.

Much to everyone's surprise, Carlton had left a will in an envelope which was found nailed to the wall inside his small and extremely modest home. Just so that there was no doubt about the contents of the envelope Carlton had written the word 'WILL' on the outside with a red, wax crayon.

There wasn't any money to leave, of course; no surprise pot of gold hidden in the dark depths of the earth closet privy, no numbered Swiss bank account and no priceless collection of paintings stored in an old trunk.

The only thing the envelope contained was £56 in well-used notes and a letter containing surprisingly detailed instructions for the disposal of his body.

The £56 was accompanied by a supplementary note confirming that this was 'to cover whatever expenses might be incurred, with whatever is left over used to buy drinks at the Duck and Puddle for all those attending the funeral'.

Heaven knows where Carlton laid his hands on £56. We were all impressed that he had managed to resist the temptation to dip into a sum that was, as far as he was concerned, the equivalent of a major lottery win.

Carlton's will made it clear that he wanted to be buried in his garden (or, more accurately, the garden of the ruined house where he had been squatting for as long as anyone could remember). That was fairly straightforward. As far as anyone of us knew (and, this being Bilbury, we weren't likely to go to the trouble of asking anyone who might really know) a citizen is perfectly entitled to have his remains buried in his own garden as long as he puts up some sort of marker so that the next generation isn't likely to come across a partly decomposed human skeleton while double digging his winter potatoes.

Indeed, being buried in your own is not an uncommon occurrence in Bilbury.

My dear friend and predecessor Dr Brownlow was buried in what was at the time his garden, and what is now the grounds of Bilbury's very own cottage hospital.

Burying Carlton in his own garden was never going to be too much of a problem (though digging a hole deep enough to take a coffin in the rocky North Devon soil was never going to be easy either), and nor was arranging for Carlton's remains to be blessed at the Church of St Damian on the outskirts of the village (that was the other main part of the instructions contained in the will).

Some time before his death Carlton had decided to ensure that the funeral could be managed as cheaply as possible. He had made the coffin himself, using an old kitchen door for the base and a few pieces of assorted plywood for the sides. The result looked rather clumsily made, it had neither been varnished nor painted and the nails which held the thing together appeared to have been hammered into place by someone with poor eyesight but plenty of enthusiasm. But it looked to be solidly made and, as things turned out, this was a good thing.

And a grave had been dug in the garden. Or, rather, it had been started. Sadly, the rocky nature of the ground meant that Carlton had not been able to dig as deep as he might have liked or, indeed, as deep as is considered normal in the grave digging world. Still, Carlton had managed to make a hole that looked like the beginnings of a grave; a shallow grave it is true, not quite deep enough to take the coffin, but a grave nevertheless. It cannot be easy to find the fire and determination to dig your own grave, especially when there is no one standing over you, with a gun, ordering you to get on with it. (I've never quite understood why people in films dig their own graves in these circumstances. Why, since the outcome is unlikely to be altered, do they not simply throw down the spade and tell the man with the gun to dig the sodding grave himself?)

It was agreed by those of us present, a sort of unofficial burial party, that if digging down another couple of feet proved impossible, particularly in ground made especially impassable as a result of recent heavy rain, then we would allow the gravedigger simply to pile earth on top of the part of the coffin that remained above ground and so create a traditional burial mound; the sort of thing was once so popular with deceased Anglo-Saxon kings.

Peter Marshall, who is, in addition to our local shopkeeper, the local undertaker, said that a burial mound would look rather nice and traditional and that he had some nice stone edging, priced very reasonably, which would look perfect with a nice little headstone which he could also lay his hands on and provide, all well within the allocated budget. His offer of a garden gnome in place of a stone angel was rejected, with thanks, even though he offered to remove the fishing rod from the gnome's hands.

Finally, Carlton, proving himself far more capable of advance planning than any of us had ever suspected, had made arrangements for his coffin to be transported between the church and his home in the breakdown truck from Tolstoy's, the local garage.

Carlton had, it seemed, done some undefined work for Reginald Westbury, the owner of the garage and the promised use of the breakdown truck had been part of the quid pro quo.

This would doubtless have worked well, for the breakdown truck had a crane at the back. The plan, apparently, was that the crane would be used to hoist Carlton's coffin onto the back of the truck.

Sadly, it was just before the 'hoisting the coffin onto the back of the truck point' in the proceedings that things started to go wrong.

The truck simply would not start.

The irony of a breakdown truck breaking down was not lost on the collected mourners, the putative congregation, and despite the solemnity of the occasion there were not a few smiles and, I regret to report, more than a few giggles.

There were plenty of people at the funeral who had vehicles large enough to carry the coffin (Thumper had his huge, extremely scruffy pick-up truck and Patchy had his van to name but two) but the garage owner, concerned that a debt is a debt until it is repaid and how else do you repay a debt to a man who has died, refused to allow anyone else to help.

Instead, Reggie insisted on using an old farm cart and the rather ancient horse which he kept on out of loyalty rather than any real sense of purpose.

The horse was, in modern parlance, well past its sell-by-date and certainly could no longer be guaranteed to produce the one horsepower which might be expected of it. It was, quite possibly, the only half a horsepower horse in the county.

Nevertheless, all would have doubtless gone without a hitch if the heavy rain which had fallen had not resulted in the stream which passes through the northern edge of the village swelling to an unusual depth. Indeed, the stream had taken on all the characteristics of a fully-fledged river rather than a meandering rural stream.

The journey to St Damian's was managed successfully.

The point where the lane crosses the stream is known, for absolutely no reason that anyone alive can recall, as Nuttock's Ford, and for twelve months of the year in nine years out of ten, the stream is no more than an inch or two deep and of little or no inconvenience to passing traffic. Motor vehicles and bicycles go through with barely a splash and the occasional pedestrians who use the lane cross, and keep their feet dry, with the aid of half a dozen strategically positioned flat stones.

However, thanks to the heavy recent rainfall, the stream had risen to a depth of six or seven inches. This was considerably greater than usual but neither the horse and cart nor the following cortege were in any way inconvenienced.

But the same was not true about the return journey.

Streams and rivers are strange things which, history shows, can sometimes change their nature in relatively short periods of time.

Back in August in 1952, the river at Lynmouth famously flooded and destroyed much of the town as it raced towards the sea.

It was, and still is, the worst river flood ever experienced in England or, indeed, any part of the United Kingdom. Over 100 buildings were destroyed and 34 people lost their lives as the River Lyn raced through the West Lyn valley. Another 420 people were made homeless and even the lighthouse was so seriously undermined that it collapsed into the river the following day.

During just a few hours, the river rose from being a picturesque attraction to being a ferocious, deadly and uncontrollable force. Within two hours, the water level rose so high that walls were broken and doors and windows smashed. A narrow point in the river became blocked with fallen trees, rocks and other debris, and when this temporary natural dam gave way the resultant rush of water caused even more damage.

That was Lynmouth in 1952.

The stream in Bilbury which crosses the lane at Nuttock's Ford is so small that it doesn't even have a name. It is regarded as quaint and rather fun, more than an inconvenience. It is so shallow that no fish could possibly survive in it.

Just how it transformed itself from such a harmless waterway into a potentially lethal river was and still is a mystery.

But, the fact is that, as luck would have it, the stream chose to become a river in the hour or so after we had crossed it on the way to St Damien's Church and before we crossed it on the way back afterwards.

I don't think anyone present realised just how deep the stream had become, nor how fast it was now flowing.

Reggie from the garage, who was sitting on the cart being pulled by the horse and who was, of course, leading the procession on its way back, just as he had the procession on its way out, certainly didn't anticipate any problems. He drove the horse forwards, thoroughly expecting to be able to drive through the swollen stream without any difficulty.

His ambition and sense of complacency were sadly misplaced.

Within a minute of entering the water, it was clear that the poor horse was struggling to cope with the rush of water. In order to save the horse from drowning, Reggie unfastened the harness and, with an agility which surprised everyone but which was inspired by an old-fashioned desire not to get his feet wet, jumped from the cart onto the horse's back.

Relieved of its heavy burden the horse and rider then safely made their way to the other bank. They, at least, had reached their destination.

When Reggie looked back from what was now the far side of the stream, he could only watch as the cart, now abandoned in the middle of the rushing water (it seems absurd to continue to describe it as a stream) was tipped over on its side.

By this time, those of us who were travelling in trucks, vans and motor cars had, of course, realised that we would stand no chance of driving through what we had to regard as a river. The water was, it was clear, far too deep even for Thumper's truck.

We all climbed out of our vehicles and stood on our side of the ford. Ironically, the sun had come out and it was quite a pleasant afternoon. Peter Marshall said loudly that it was a lovely day to be buried.

We then all watched in horror as Carlton's coffin was swept off the cart, down the river and out of sight. The cart, too wide to be swept away, lay on its side, being battered by the water and slowly breaking up. The coffin, just the right size to float downstream, swung gracefully and naturally into a position best suited for its new situation, and disappeared between the trees and bushes which normally mark the boundaries of the stream.

There then followed much discussion as we all tried to work out exactly where the stream went and where the coffin was likely to end up. It was generally agreed that the stream, which wriggles and turns in the unpredictable way of streams everywhere, would, even in its new swollen state, pass through several of Mr Kennett's fields before joining forces with another, larger and also unnamed stream which eventually led down to the sea.

Thumper, who had been following directly behind the horse and cart, leapt back into his vehicle and called for the rest of us to join him. And so Anne, the mother of Thumper's children, together with Patchy, Peter Marshall and me all climbed into or onto Thumper's truck as he turned left through an open gate and began the drive along a muddy field in an attempt to follow the path of the stream.

It was, to say the least, a bumpy and slightly unnerving journey and I like to think that Carlton, who was something of a wild spirit and, in his modest way, an adventurer manqué, would have enjoyed the experience. Indeed, I like to think that he enjoyed his final nautical voyage as captain and crew of his small, homemade vessel.

As Thumper drove the truck, the rest of us struggled to keep an eye on the coffin in case it caught on a branch or grounded, as we constantly expected it to do.

But for a mile or so the coffin did neither of these things. It sailed proudly on the waters and we were all impressed at Carlton's skill in managing to construct a coffin which had proved surprisingly seaworthy. All it really needed, said Patchy, was a Jolly Roger flag flying proudly from the prow.

We followed that darned coffin for hours and it travelled for miles.

Actually, it didn't of course.

It just felt like it.

But we did follow the coffin for a third of mile and for twenty minutes. Every time we thought it had caught on a tree root or a rock the damned thing managed to free itself and carry on floating along with the river.

Eventually, we caught up with it, of course.

We never really thought that the coffin would end up being washed out to sea, although Peter Marshall, in a gloomy mood, for he was in charge of the interment and had a grave digger standing by with spade and stone edging ready for action, did predict that the coffin would disappear into the Bristol Channel and that Carlton's body would probably be washed ashore somewhere along the Welsh coast, much to the confusion and bemusement of the Welsh constabulary.

Much to our relief, the coffin eventually stopped travelling when it was caught against a weir near to Huddle Stone Cottage, a tiny one bedroomed home miles from any neighbours and normally reached only by an always overgrown cart track.

After Thumper screeched to a halt and we all piled out of the truck, the owner of the cottage, an elderly gentleman called Albert Perry, came out to see what all the fuss was about.

He had been enjoying a late lunch or an early dinner for he had a spoon in one hand and a bowl of something steaming hot in the other. We were all on the other side of the stream from him and from where the coffin had come to rest.

'Hullo, Mr Perry,' I called, 'I'm sorry to bother you but do you think we could have our coffin back, please?'

'Has it got a body in it?'

'It has,' I agreed.

Mr Perry looked at us and then at the coffin, bobbing by the bank near to the weir. 'Who's in it?' he called back.

'Carlton,' I shouted, 'Carlton Tregallon.'

'Don't know him,' said Mr Perry. 'Never heard of him. You can have him back. I got no use for a coffin with a body in it. Specially not for a body I ain't never heard of.'

And with that he went back indoors to finish his meal. I often wonder what he would have said if the coffin had been occupied by someone he knew.

Thumper had to drive for another two miles to find a place where he could cross the stream and then two miles back to Mr Perry's cottage.

It took all of us nearly an hour to drag the coffin out of the water and into the back of Thumper's truck. And then, since Peter's gravedigger was waiting at Carlton's place, and being paid by the hour, Peter insisted that we drive straight to the grave and see Carlton buried before Thumper took us back to where we had left all our other vehicles.

The rest of the ceremony went without alarums or excursions.

We buried Carlton, and Peter's man fitted the stones around the mound of earth that marked the spot. It didn't look a bad place to be buried to be honest with you. Peter, who said he knew where he could lay his hands on something second-hand at a very reasonable price, promised to put a stone cross on the site to mark the spot.

And then Thumper took us back to where our cars were parked and we all went to the Duck and Puddle to say goodbye to Carlton in the time honoured manner.

After Peter had told us what his bill was there wasn't much money left, of course. But there was enough for us all to wet our whistles, and so we saw old Carlton off in modest but enthusiastic style.

He'd lived an unusual life had old Carlton and I think it's fair to say that his passing was a little out of the ordinary too. The funny thing is that although I hardly knew him I will miss him. He was one of life's characters and there aren't enough of those around these days.

When I got back to Bilbury Grange, I was exhausted but not tired. It's funny, but there is a difference. I realised that I ought to write to Beryl Tregallon to let her know that she was a widow. But I thought the letter could probably wait an hour or so. And so I poured myself a Laphroig as a nightcap, took the bottle with me and slumped down into my favourite chair. Patsy brought over a jug of water and added a little water to the whisky. I looked at the glass.

'Have I put in too much water?' she asked.

'I'll add a drop more whisky,' I said.

I think Patsy does that thing with the water deliberately. If she thinks I need a decent drink she puts in a little too much water so that I have to make the necessary adjustments.

She smiled at me. 'You look as if you need it.'

I did indeed. It had been a busy day.

The Bus Shelter (Without a Bus)

The Bilbury bus shelter (we only have one in the village and so it is a source of considerable pride) has been in need of repair and restoration for some time and a kind but misguided resident, who will remain anonymous (largely because no one but the person concerned knows their identity), telephoned the local council and pointed out to them that the roof leaks and so the shelter does not live up to its name. The call was, I gather, made around nine months ago. The bus shelter is made entirely of wood and has a thatched roof. It was, according to Patsy's father who knew the men who built it, put up in the 1930s. It has a wooden bench inside and a wooden floor and if the village had a regular bus service it would be an excellent place in which to sit and wait for a bus to arrive. But the roof, which has needed re-thatching for some time, leaks rather badly.

Six months ago, a team of workmen arrived in Bilbury.

There were six of them and they came in two lorries. They were accompanied by a man in a small, white van. The man in the small, white van wore a cheap, ill-fitting suit, the sort you can buy from the sale rack at a discount clothing stall, a white, transparent nylon shirt which shone, and almost glowed, with whiteness, and a hideous kipper tie which had clearly been designed by a colour blind child who'd been given a brush and too many paints. This seventh man was clearly very important because he had six or seven pens in his top jacket pocket.

I knew they had arrived in the village because they got lost and the man in the van, who was leading the procession, called at Bilbury Grange and asked for directions.

'It says here that the shelter is in Totterdown Lane,' said the man, showing me a piece of paper which said, in clear black type, that the bus shelter was in Totterdown Lane.

'It is,' I agreed.

'But where is Totterdown Lane?' demanded the man. 'There aren't any road signs around.' He said this as though he were holding me personally responsible for the failure of adequate signage in the village.

'There aren't any road signs in Bilbury,' I told him. 'But to get to Totterdown Lane you just need to go straight along Potter's Lane, turn left into the lane by Softly's Bottom, take the first right into a lane which, as far as I know, does not have a name, and then you'll find Totterdown Lane on the left.'

The man stared at me as if I'd just given him instructions in Latin.

They only had to travel half a mile so I got out my bicycle and showed them the way. Leading a small procession of vehicles made me feel very important. I was in the lead, pedalling quietly, and behind me came the white van and then the two lorries laden with men and materials. I thought we must have looked quite impressive, needing only a police escort to be very impressive.

'Ah,' said the man in the suit, when I proudly showed them the bus shelter which was the purpose of their visit. He frowned and shook his head as though rather shocked and disappointed. 'This will need a 548/12. And we'll need to obtain a Restructuring Allocation which will necessitate a Planning Officer Rural Recommitment Intervention.' He spoke in a way which made it clear which words began with capital letters.

'What's a 548/12?' I asked.

'A full road closure,' explained the man in the suit, who seemed startled that there could be a human being anywhere who didn't know what a 548/12 might be. 'There's nowhere for us to park while we do the work and so we'll need permission for a cessation of traffic order. We'll have to speak to the Highways Planner and the police. We'll need temporary redirection signs erecting and traffic lights and a portable generator putting into place. And there will need to be a site inspection by proper authorities.'

'It's just a bus shelter,' I said. 'The roof needs re-thatching.'

The man stared at me, aghast. 'The current structure in its present configuration does not satisfy health and safety requirements or meet the required building standard specifications,' he said pompously. I looked at the bus shelter and felt sorry for it.

That was six months ago and I'd forgotten all about the bus shelter, the workmen and the man in the cheap suit.

But they came back.

And they came back in force.

This time the man in the white van was accompanied by four large lorries, a crane, a JCB digger, twelve workmen and a huge amount of equipment. They came with temporary traffic lights, lots of red signs saying ROAD CLOSED and lots of yellow signs which had DIVERSION printed on them. They brought enough scaffolding to cover the Eiffel Tower, two portable toilet cabins and a small administrative building which was bigger than the village bus shelter and which came on the back of its own lorry.

They came first to Bilbury Grange so that I could once again lead them to the bus shelter. I'm afraid that this time they had to wait while I finished my morning surgery. I did draw them a little map on the back of an old envelope but the man in the cheap suit, who still had the requisite number of pens in his jacket breast pocket, said that they would prefer to wait and be led to the site by what he called a 'knowledgeable local resident'. He said that the last time they had been in the village it had taken them four hours to find their way back to Barnstaple and that he didn't want to spend the rest of the day driving round looking for the bus shelter.

When I had completed the surgery and went out to take them round to the bus shelter I found that while they'd been waiting, they had entertained themselves by making several gallons of tea and cooking bacon and eggs on what looked to me like a camping stove but what was, I am sure, more accurately known as an 'Approved Portable Food Preparation Apparatus'. The men were sitting on folding chairs, eating, drinking and reading their newspapers. The British workman at work can be a magnificent sight.

It took the men 45 minutes to make the necessary preparations to continue their journey. There was much grumbling because they had settled in and were clearly not expecting to have to move. The toilet cabin which had been lifted off the back of its lorry had to be lifted back on again and the 'Approved Portable Food Preparation Apparatus' had to be packed up and put back into its proper place. And, of course, all the tea had to be drunk and all the bacon and egg sandwiches had to be consumed.

This time I led them round to the bus shelter in the Rolls Royce, simply because I had a couple of calls to make and one of the calls was to a village about three miles away. So the procession consisted of a Rolls Royce followed by three large lorries, followed by a digger, followed by a crane, followed by another large lorry, followed by the man in the white van who this time somehow managed to get himself at the end of the procession.

I showed them the bus shelter and then, as they began to unload their lorries, I carried on to do my morning calls. Before I left I could not help noticing that the first things they took off the lorries were the tea making equipment and the 'Approved Portable Food Preparation Apparatus'. Then came the folding chairs and the portable toilet. These were clearly workers who had their priorities sorted out properly.

I had a busy day at the surgery and a number of calls to do around the village and consequently I didn't think anything more about the bus shelter. I simply assumed that the gang of workmen had done the necessary repairs and gone on their way.

However, a few days later I received an alarming telephone call from a villager called Taunton Trelawney.

Taunton is a normally genial man in what is usually known diplomatically in the late autumn of his life. He is long retired but used to be an architect in a large practice in Exeter. He carved a pleasant niche for himself as the firm's premier designer of bespoke garages and summer houses. He and his wife bought a cottage in Bilbury when they were both in their 40s and it was always their intention to retire to the village in the fullness of time. The cottage was, I gather, rather run down and quite a bargain.

'It's not often you get a once-in-a-lifetime opportunity,' said Mr Trelawney, when telling me about their purchase.

And so, when the calendar ticked round, and it became time to do so, the Trelawneys did precisely as they had planned and became permanent residents in the village.

Mrs Trelawney is, despite her years, a keen tennis player and an enthusiastic member of a local rambling club. She has a large bosom, which looks rather like a jib sail in a full gale, and when she walks into a room the bosom always arrives a moment or two before the rest of her. She's a bubbly sort of woman who likes talking.

'I've had a good many lovers,' she once said. 'How many do you think?'

'Now, what sort of question is that?' I said. I have no idea what triggered the question and I had no idea what the correct answer might be. Nor did I have any idea what would be a tactful number to suggest. When she pushed me, I said 'three' because it sounded enough to show experience and not enough to suggest that she had been a woman of easy virtue.

'Twenty two!' she said, with pride. 'Enough for two entire football teams! But none of them as good in bed as my husband. He was very strict when we were younger. I once burnt the pudding when we had guests and he put me over his knee, hoiked up my dress and spanked me in front of everyone. They were all very shocked but I enjoyed it enormously and was always waiting for him to do it again.' She paused, and thought and then smiled. 'I can't think how many puddings I burnt after that,' she said, wistfully. 'But he never did it again,' she added, sadly.

I confess that this unsolicited knowledge stayed with me, resting out of sight at the back of my mind, but it always came to the forefront when I saw either of them. I saw Mr Trelawney, with his bathukolpian wife over his knee. And I saw Mrs Trelawney burning puddings.

As far as I know, the only ailment Mrs Trelawney has had in the years since I've been her GP has been a verruca, a simple warty disorder which is almost as difficult to spell as it is to treat successfully. She also suffers a little from deafness, but she refuses any help for that.

At the time of the second bus shelter incident, I had been treating it for several months and progress had been slow.

Her visits to the surgery were not speedy either.

She always came well encased in garments which seemed to have been designed with safety in mind. Whatever the weather she always wore a corset strong enough to withstand point blank fire from a .38 pistol. The corset was fitted with industrial strength suspender straps which looked as if they could have been used to tether a barrage balloon in a gale. Whenever she visited and I asked her to remove the appropriate stocking she always expressed surprise, as though the very idea that I would need her to remove clothing in order to examine her verruca was something of a shock. She would then insist on going behind the screen and removing not just the stocking but also the corset. The whole process of disrobing took so long that from time to time I would call out to ask if everything was going smoothly. I lived in fear that one day I would sit and wait, and wait, and eventually move aside the screen and see Mrs Trelawney lying on the floor, deceased, and probably still wearing her damned corset.

And while I was toying with her verruca she would talk. And talk, and talk.

She once asked my advice about her collection of porcelain frogs.

'I've got hundreds of the damned things,' she told me. 'I hate them but everyone buys them for me at birthdays and at Christmas. My husband bought me one several years ago and, being polite, I said I liked it, as you do, and so he bought me another one for our anniversary and then a third for Christmas and it just sort of got out of hand. I know what I'll get for Christmas. Another bloody frog. How do I stop people buying them for me?'

I told her that when her husband next gave her a china frog she should admire it and then tell him that he could never find a better one and so she wanted this one to be the last he ever bought. And I suggested that she tell relatives and friends that the china frog collecting was now over.

She was very pleased with that advice, though I don't know if she tried it and if she did, whether it worked or not.

As the weeks went by, I suggested that she might visit a chiropodist in Barnstaple but she insisted on allowing me the privilege of tackling her verruca.

Mr Trelawney is also in decent health. He is a keen rambler, though he suffers from mild angina and moderate high blood pressure. As long as he does not get too excited both these problems seem to be well under control.

He also has a good deal of hair growing out of his nostrils, probably more than is considered appropriate in most polite circles, but neither he nor Mrs Trelawney has ever noticed this profusion or else he has decided to let nature takes its course. He once shared my waiting room with Mrs Blackmore and Nigel, her six-year-old. Nigel would not stop crying and only after I had sat him down in my surgery and given him a lollipop would he admit that he had been terrified of the man with spiders up his nose.

Mr Trelawney would be the first to admit that he is not the brightest bulb in the chandelier, probably no more than a 20 watt would be my guess, and during his professional career, he never made the mistake of trying to stretch beyond his capabilities – hence his decision to concentrate on designing garages and summerhouses.

But he is a good, kind, honest man who cares. Those may be generally regarded these days as rather out of favour qualities; a little old-fashioned in the wider world maybe, but in Bilbury those are still respected as important qualities.

Mr Trelawney telephoned me a day or two after the second visit of the men from the council.

'It's gone!' he said Mr Trelawney.

I didn't have to ask him who was speaking because Mr Trelawney has a unique way of shouting. As a result of his wife's deafness, and her refusal to wear a hearing aid of any kind (or even to use a speaking trumpet), he has permanently turned up his personal volume and so is sometimes invited to compere local events where the organisers are unable to afford a loudspeaker system, or even to rent a loud hailer.

'That's good,' I said. 'They can be difficult to shift sometimes.'

'Well this one was easy enough to move!' replied Mr Trelawney. He sounded in a bad mood and I wondered why he could possibly be upset that his wife's verruca had disappeared. I was also slightly puzzled by his remark that moving it had been 'easy' since Mrs Trelawney and I had been battling with the darned thing for several months.

'The important thing is to make sure that it doesn't come back,' I said.

'I'm damned sure it's not coming back!' said Mr Trelawney. 'You should see the monstrosity which has appeared in its place.'

'Oh dear,' I said. 'It sounds as if I'd better take a look. Can your wife pop along this evening?'

'Why the hell do you need my wife there?'

'It'll be difficult to do anything without her!' I laughed.

'What do expect her to do?' demanded Mr Trelawney.

'Just slip off her stockings and jump up on the examination couch.'

Mr Trelawney made a noise like the pressure cooker my mother used to have when I was a boy. It was a fairly early model and the steam release valve was rather temperamental. 'And then what do you intend to do?'

'Well, I'll just take a good look!'

Mr Trelawney repeated his excellent impersonation of a pressure cooker with steam escaping. 'I rang you because I thought you'd be sympathetic and offer some useful advice,' he said at last. 'I certainly didn't expect to have to listen to this sort of filth.'

I paused and thought for a moment. 'How do you expect me to deal with your wife's verruca if I don't have a good look at it?'

'Verruca? What verruca?'

'The one on your wife's foot.'

'Oh, I'm not interested in that,' said Mr Trelawney, dismissively.

I was puzzled. 'Then what are we talking about?'

'The bus shelter.'

'The village bus shelter?'

'Of course.' He sighed. 'Why would I ring you up to talk about a bus shelter in Northampton?'

'Have they finished the repairs?' I asked.

'No, they haven't,' replied Mr Trelawney angrily. 'They've torn the damned thing down and put up some monstrosity made of plastic and steel.'

After a few more minutes of conversation with Mr Trelawney I managed to discover that instead of repairing the old bus shelter, the wooden one with the thatched roof, the council workmen had torn the building down and replaced it with a hideous modern structure made of sheets of plastic, held together with monstrous steel struts.

'Instead of a proper seat there's a funny little piece of red plastic that people are supposed to lean on!' said Mr Trelawney. He now sounded as if he were about to burst into tears.

Prevention of serious illness is an important part of any doctor's job and it seemed to me that if I didn't do something there was a good chance that Mr Trelawney would have some sort of vascular accident – a heart attack or a stroke. So I told him to meet me at the bus shelter in five minutes time.

I arrived first and I was shocked at what I saw.

Mr Trelawney was absolutely right.

The council workmen had dismantled and taken away the old, original bus shelter and had replaced it with some space age creation which would have probably looked at home on an interplanetary space mission station but which looked distinctly out of place in Bilbury.

'We've got to do something about it!' said Mr Trelawney.

'I wonder what happened to the original one,' I said, not truly expecting him to know.

'The council workmen smashed it up and dumped all the bits on the tip,' explained Mr Trelawney. 'I telephoned them before I telephoned you.'

I thought about it for a moment. 'We need a Bus Shelter Action Committee,' I said. 'You ring up everyone you know and I'll ring up some people. We'll tell everyone that we'll meet in the Duck and Puddle tomorrow evening. Tell everyone you ring to try to have a look at the new bus shelter so that they know what we're talking about.'

And so the following evening, a couple of dozen of us gathered in the snug at the Duck and Puddle. Thumper Robinson and Patchy Fogg were there, together with Mr Kennett, Patsy's father, and several other local farmers. Mr Trelawney had brought along several of his neighbours. We all agreed that the new bus shelter just wouldn't do. And we all agreed that if we couldn't have our old bus shelter back then we wanted something pretty well identical.

'We could contact the council, tell them we aren't happy with the wretched thing they've put up and demand that they replace it with something more in-keeping with Bilbury's rural environment,' said Mr Trelawney.

'Good idea!' said Gilly Parsons, the publican's wife and the chef, chief barmaid, senior bottle washer and joint proprietor of the Granny Kennett Pudding Club at the Duck and Puddle. Gilly is always ready for a fight with bureaucrats.

'I'm afraid I don't think that will do any good,' said Patchy, sadly. 'Now that they've put up a new shelter they'll say we have to make do with what we have been given.' He shrugged. 'That's their way.'

It was Thumper who came up with the answer. 'We'll take down the new thing they've put up and get rid of it. And then we'll rebuild the old bus shelter.'

'Will they let us do that?' asked Mr Trelawney, uncertainly.

'Of course, not!' said Thumper. 'So we won't tell them what we're doing. We'll get rid of their horrible new thing and put up something nice and rustic of our own.'

It was generally agreed that no one at the council would ever notice that we had changed the nature of the bus shelter. Very few officials or politicians ever visit Bilbury. And if they do come they invariably get lost in our maze of unlabelled lanes. Most maps of this part of North Devon are useless. The vast majority of maps don't include details of many of our narrow lanes and I have seen a number of maps and atlases which don't even acknowledge the existence of the village Bilbury.

Moreover, if, perchance, a stranger from the big city of Barnstaple were to notice our bus shelter, it would never occur to them that it wasn't the same bus shelter that had been erected some years earlier – by the council.

'It'll cost a pretty penny,' warned Mr Kennett.

'We'll raise the money somehow,' said Thumper.

'I'll draw up the plans for free!' offered Mr Trelawney.

Patchy ordered more drinks and we sat around for half an hour working out how to get the work done and how to find the cash to pay for it. Mr Trelawney was appointed architect and project manager.

No one else mentioned it so I thought I ought to point out, just in case anyone thought it relevant, that in the latest issue of the local paper it was reported that the local bus company was halting the weekly bus service to Bilbury on the grounds that the route was uneconomical. I made this point as everyone sipped and thought of ways to raise the money for the replacement for the replacement bus shelter.

'What's that got to do with anything?' demanded Mr Trelawney. 'The old bus shelter was a beautiful little building. We owe it to the next generation to restore it to its former glory.'

'That old bus shelter was a handy little building before it started leaking,' said Thumper. 'It's quite close to the river. On a wet day I often popped in there to eat my sandwiches while I was out fishing.' He looked around. 'Sandwiches go all soggy in the rain,' he explained.

'My wife found it useful if she'd been into the village,' said another one of the farmers. 'If she had heavy shopping from Peter Marshall's shop she would stop there for a sit and a rest on her way home.'

So the Bus Shelter Action Committee duly decided that we would erect, or arrange to have erected, a new wooden bus shelter with a thatched roof and that we, the Action Committee, would find a way to fund the building.

That's the way we like to do things in Bilbury.

Just because there are no buses doesn't mean that you can't have a damned good looking bus shelter.

Just Before Dawn

I've never really worked out how many night calls I deal with. Sometimes I can go for a whole week without getting up at night. At other times, the night calls seem to come thick and fast. Occasionally, I have had to get up three or four times in a single night.

Night calls are often particularly memorable and, since the villagers of Bilbury are, by and large, a sensible lot who only call for help when they really need it, I genuinely don't mind getting up in the middle of the night. It's my job and I like doing it. Night calls can be enormously rewarding and I feel sorry for those doctors who, for one reason or another, don't ever do them. (There are always one or two unreasonable patients who will request night time calls without consideration. But the annoyance caused by these patients is far outweighed by the genuine, professional satisfaction of being to help someone in pain or fear.)

When I received a telephone call asking me to go and see Oliver Windle I knew that I needed to move quickly. Oliver suffers from asthma and as far as I am concerned if he has a fault it is that he tends to wait too long before calling for help. He takes tablets and has an inhaler but sometimes his wheezing just gets out of control.

It was, I suppose, about two in the morning, early one April, when the call came in from his wife. She told me that Oliver was wheezing badly and that he'd been in trouble since the early evening. He'd refused to let her call me earlier but now she felt that he definitely needed help – and needed it rather urgently. He'd tried everything that normally did the trick – even drinking two cups of very strong black coffee.

I got dressed quickly, picked up my black bag and a small oxygen cylinder which I keep in the surgery for such emergencies, and set off out into the night.

Most of the time we never really know people the first time we meet them because we probably only see the person they want us to think they are. But Oliver was different. What you saw was what you got for he never changed.

Oliver had been named after the fat half of Laurel and Hardy because his mother, who had clearly not done enough research into the matter, mistakenly thought that Oliver was the name of the thin half of the duo, the one who had been born in the Lake District in the North of England. In fact, of course, Oliver was the plump one who was born in Georgia, US.

Oliver's parents had enjoyed a very pleasant honeymoon in the Lake District and that was where Oliver had been conceived. If Oliver had been born a girl he would have probably been called Beatrix after Beatrix Potter, the author who lived in the Lake District. And if his parents had paid closer attention to the identities of the two stars of the Laurel and Hardy movies, he would have been named Stan.

Oliver was not, it is fair to say, the brightest of God's creatures and Thumper, who knew him well, always said he had a brain power which put him somewhere between that of a ferret and a cockatoo. Patchy said that his literary skills were such that he would have had a hard time if faced with a one letter anagram. None of this was said unkindly or with malice. Oliver himself readily admitted that he could never tackle a sum involving a total larger than his available complement of fingers and thumbs.

For most of those who are limited to using digital help with their arithmetic, this limitation means that sums of up to ten are perfectly possible, but in Oliver's case the limit had been reduced to eight. He had lost the middle and index fingers of his right hand while endeavouring to remove a tuft of grass blocking the blade of a petrol-driven lawnmower. Sadly, he had attempted to carry out this simple procedure without taking the precaution of turning off the engine. The moment the blockage was removed, the blade had resumed its twirling faster than Oliver had been able to remove his hand.

It is perfectly possible that it would have been feasible to reattach the severed digits had Oliver had the presence of mind to seek medical help with some degree of urgency. However, he delayed for nearly 24 hours before seeking advice. This was some time before he married and he alone must take full responsibility for the delay.

After the accident, Oliver wrapped his hand in a grubby handkerchief and put the two severed fingers into the hip pocket of his jeans. By the time he finally arrived in my surgery, it was all that medicine could do to save his infected hand. The fingers, which had been crushed (he had sat on them while watching television) were almost unrecognisable as human and the vicar and Oliver later gave them a Christian burial in an unused corner of the churchyard.

I should mention, as an aside, that losing fingers is something of a local pastime in North Devon. My guess is that the average complement of fingers and thumbs in the area is something only slightly larger than nine.

When I asked him why he hadn't come to see me sooner, Oliver explained the delay by pointing out that there had been a football match on the television that evening and that he had been looking forward to watching it for the best part of a week.

Oliver is a tireless hard worker who never seems to feel pain or weariness in the way the rest of us do. Although he doesn't work on a farm, he is good with animals and I once saw him intimidate an enraged and aggressive bull simply by standing and staring at it. He is brave and kind and does not have a malicious thought in his head. But he is certainly not a man you would hire to take an IQ test for you if success at that endeavour were important to you. I cannot think of anyone else I have ever known who would put two severed fingers into their pocket and then forget about them for 24 hours.

Oliver is, for reasons lost in the mists of time, known to everyone as 'Boy'.

It is how he still refers to himself, even though he is now a married man in his early sixties. He always refers to himself in the third person as in 'Boy doesn't like damsons' or 'Boy had a good win on the horses last week'. I've no idea why he does this. It certainly isn't out of affectation or arrogance, as it is with some of the celebrities who do it.

Boy had an informal training as a car mechanic (no paperwork was involved at any stage) and he works for Tolstoy's, the local garage, where he looks after many of the vehicles in the village. Dr Brownlow was an enthusiastic supporter and always asked that Oliver take care of routine servicing of his elderly Rolls Royce. I continue that tradition.

'When you take your car to the garage for a service the first thing they do is fiddle with everything,' Dr Brownlow once complained. 'They change the seat position, move the driving mirror, retune the radio and generally make a real mess of everything. Boy never does any of that.'

When seatbelts were introduced, Oliver was reluctant to fit them unless ordered to do so. He claimed it was because he couldn't work out how to fix them to the bodywork but I never believed that story. I think he thought they were unsightly. He and I were at one about seatbelts. I know I should have had seatbelts put into the car when they were introduced but I get in and out of the car all day long and I know I would get all tangled up, and probably break my neck, if I had belts in the car. I'm sure they'll make them compulsory eventually and when they do I'll have them fitted. Maybe very old cars such as the Rolls will be exempt.

When he was 52-years-old, Oliver got married to a lovely lady called Sheila. He and his new bride sold the house he'd inherited from his parents and Oliver explained that the stairs were getting too much for him. He has arthritis in both knees as well as the asthma. He and Sheila bought a bungalow which he said would be much easier to manage. I remember being rather surprised at his choice of bungalow for the property he bought could only be accessed after climbing a long flight of steps from the lane.

'Won't the steps be a problem for you?' I asked him.

He shook his head. 'It's only stairs I have trouble with,' he said. 'I can manage steps outside with no bother.'

When I arrived at the bungalow in response to Sheila's urgent telephone call, the front door was open and Sheila was standing waiting for me. She'd seen and heard my car approaching and she had the front door open before I'd started climbing the steps.

Oliver was sitting in an easy chair in the front room and he was definitely struggling. He was in the early stages of status asthmaticus – a dangerous and potentially deadly condition for asthma sufferers. Status asthmaticus is always unresponsive to all the usual bronchodilators. Sometimes the air passages go into spasm and, when narrowed, become plugged with mucus. It is a frightening condition – frightening for both sufferer and observers alike.

Oliver was clutching an inhaler in one hand and holding his chest with the other. A bottle of the tablets he used was on a small table by his side. He looked like death and my first thought was that I was going to have a fight on my hands to keep him alive.

'Has anything unusual happened recently?' I asked his wife.

'He had a bad cold,' she told me, 'but you know what he's like. He doesn't like to bother you. He always thinks he can deal with things by himself.'

'Next time he's poorly you decide whether or not to call me,' I told her firmly.

Sheila nodded and promised that she would.

I got the oxygen cylinder set up and fitted a mask on Oliver's face. I hoped that the oxygen supply would help reduce the hypoxemia from which he was suffering.

'He'll be all right won't he, doctor?' asked Shelia. I knew that she had never seen him in such a bad way.

'Of course he will,' I said, with more confidence than I felt. 'But it's a good job you didn't wait any longer to call me.'

I opened my black bag and took out a syringe, a needle and a vial of a powerful corticosteroid.

'Oliver wanted me to wait until daylight to call you,' said Sheila.

I looked at her. 'Well, I'm glad you didn't.'

I didn't tell Sheila, of course, but if she had waited then we would have had to call the undertaker.

I quickly found a vein and injected the steroid straight into Oliver's arm. The oxygen was already beginning to make a difference and his colour was improving.

As I knelt beside him, waiting for the steroid to start to work and the wheezing to be reduced, I couldn't help thinking how often it is that really serious health problems occur at this time of the night.

All living things operate according to an internal clock and human beings are no exception. It has been known for centuries that the leaves of some plants regularly open during the daytime and close at night. It was always assumed that this phenomenon was a response to sunlight. But over two 250 years ago, in 1729, a French astronomer called Jean-Jacques de Mairan, conducted a very simple experiment which showed that this assumption was wrong. He discovered that this phenomenon occurs even if a plant is kept in the dark. The only possible explanation was that the plant opens and closes in response to some sort of 24-hour internal clock. That was the first experiment in chronobiology.

Since then, chronobiology (the study of temporal patterns related to biological phenomena) has become an acknowledged science. It is now known that just about every living organism, from a nucleated single cell to a human being, follows a 24-hour or circadian rhythm.

So, for example, a human being's pulse rate and blood pressure are highest first thing in the morning (with the result that the incidence of heart attacks and strokes is highest at that time of day). In the evening, the pulse rate and blood pressure will naturally fall. The human body temperature rises during the day and falls at night. The body's blood platelets, which help with blood clotting, are stickier in the morning than at any other time of day. A man is, therefore, likely to have less trouble with bleeding if he nicks himself shaving in the morning than if he nicks himself in the evening. The human tolerance for alcohol peaks at five o'clock in the afternoon. And finally, most babies are born, and most people die, between the hours of midnight and dawn.

Our bodies respond in a cyclical way because we have evolved on earth, and the amount of light and heat, and the level of electromagnetic and gravitational forces, all vary in a rhythmic way.

The important thing, still widely ignored by doctors, is that the abnormalities associated with disease also vary in a cyclical and circadian way.

Whether a patient is suffering from asthma, cancer, heart disease or arthritis, their disease will change during the day and, consequently, whatever is done to tackle the disease should also be arranged according to a circadian rhythm.

For example, the body's ability to absorb drugs varies a good deal throughout the day. When given at the right time of day, a drug will have a powerful and positive effect on an illness. But when given at the wrong time of day, a drug may prove toxic. All this is known but surprisingly few doctors take no notice of any of it.

I find the way the body changes during the day and the night truly fascinating, and I was thinking about this unrecognised branch of medicine while I waited for Oliver to recover. I was confident that if I could keep him alive until daybreak then he would make a good recovery.

Asthma is one of the commonest diseases in the world. And it is getting commoner. The disease has been so widely investigated that we know that because of the circadian rhythms associated with a number of normal physiological processes (such as airway size and breathing patterns) the majority of asthma attacks take place between 2.00 a.m. and 6.00 a.m. in the morning. The airways are naturally open widest during the day and there is a reduction in airflow after midnight.

Knowing all this, I firmly believed that if I could keep Oliver alive until sunrise then he would be over the worst, and he would survive.

Slowly, steadily and undeniably I watched Oliver's condition improve.

As the minutes ticked by so the wheezing eased and his colour improved. Soon he was able to speak. His wife felt comfortable enough to leave the room to fill the kettle and to make us all a cup of tea.

Typically, the first thing Oliver said, when he finally had enough breath to talk, was to apologise for my being called out.

'I wanted to wait until the morning,' he said.

It's funny how some people are like that. Some patients will call the doctor out at the drop of a hat, telephoning at 3.00 a.m. on Christmas morning because they've run out of cream for their athlete's foot. But others will refuse to call for help, waiting for morning, waiting for Monday, waiting for things to get better by themselves.

I told Oliver that his wife had been right to call me. And I told him firmly that I had given her authority to call me whenever she thought I was needed – and not to wait until he was ready to call.

As the minutes ticked by, so Oliver grew stronger. Soon he was out of danger. I told him I would leave the oxygen cylinder with him but that I didn't think he would need it again. I also told his wife that she had to call me if there was any deterioration but that I would call in later that day to see how he was. There was some sign of infection in his chest and I decided to start him on a week's course of an antibiotic. Drugs in the antibiotic group are, in my view, prescribed far too often. It is one of the reasons why there are now so many dangerous infections which are immune to antibiotics. But there are times when antibiotics are essential and this was one of them.

I left Oliver and Sheila just after dawn.

The drive back home was magnificent.

The sun was rising over the hills and the sky was showing signs that we were going to have a good day.

My route took me past the new Bilbury bus shelter which had been finished just that week. It had a thatched roof and a wooden seat inside. No buses stopped there but we had the best damned bus shelter in Devon. Looking at the shelter which Mr Trelawney had designed and the village had built made me smile with pride.

The drive home was made all that much better because I knew that I had actually made a difference. You can't often say that in life so the moments when you can are worth cherishing.

I made a slight detour and drove past the Little Hampton cricket ground on my way home. As I went past, I slowed for a few moments to look at the empty pavilion and the neatly mown square. I felt that winter was truly over and spring was definitely here.

When I got back to Bilbury Grange I was feeling good.

Patsy was still asleep and there was no point at all in waking her.

I paused for a moment; unsure whether to go back to bed or to make breakfast.

Eventually, I decided that I wouldn't sleep if I did go back to bed, so I fed Ben and made myself breakfast.

When the kettle had boiled and the eggs were ready I put on a coat, arranged my feast on a tray and took the tray outside to eat in the early morning sunshine. Two boiled eggs with slices of fresh bread, buttered and cut into 'soldiers', a plateful of toast, lashings of home-made marmalade, a glass of pineapple juice and a huge pot of coffee.

Outside, it wasn't warm but it wasn't cold either. I sat on a wooden chair at our wooden garden table. Ben, who had finished his breakfast and had found an old bone, chewed happily beneath my feet. There was a mist over the garden and I could see the sun starting to shine through it. The grass was wet with dew. The birds were already up and about and were singing merrily to welcome another day.

I'd missed my sleep but it didn't matter a damn for life felt very, very good.

For the umpteenth time I told myself how lucky I was to be working in Bilbury.

There really is no place quite like it.

Appendix 1

The Doc's List of Things People Achieved After the Age of 65

At the age of 66
Colonel Sanders started Kentucky Fried Chicken and by the time he was 70 had 400 franchise restaurants; John Betjeman became Poet Laureate; Edgar Rice Burroughs, author of the Tarzan books, became a war correspondent

At the age of 67
Josephine Baker, the dancer, made a return to the Broadway stage; Tolstoy rode a bicycle for the first time in his life; John Dryden, the poet, agreed to supply a publisher with 10,000 verses for £300; Simeon Poisson discovered the laws of probability (after studying the chances of French army personnel being killed by mule kicks)

At the age of 68
Queen Victoria started to learn Hindustani; Sir C Aubrey Smith, the former England cricket captain, made his first movie in Hollywood; Mrs Patrick Campbell, the actress, also made her first film

At the age of 69
Ronald Reagan was elected President of the United States of America; Noah Webster published his eponymous dictionary; Gilbert White published the *Natural History of Selborne*

At the age of 70
Francis Galton invented the science of finger printing; Alfred Wallis, a Cornish fisherman in St Ives, began to paint and duly made both himself and St Ives world famous; Copernicus published *The Revolutions of Heavenly Bodies*; Enid Blyton wrote 11 books in the year; Hilda Johnstone became a competitor in the Olympics, taking

part in the equestrian dressage competition; Maurice Chevalier starred in the film Gigi and sang 'Thank heavens for Little Girls'

At the age of 71
Coco Chanel designed the Chanel suit; Leni Riefenstahl, the filmmaker, took up scuba diving; Katsusuke Yanagisawa, a retired Japanese schoolteacher, climbed Mount Everest

At the age of 72
Karl Wallenda walked a tightrope between the top floors of two hotels in Miami; Colette wrote Gigi; Jomo Kenyatta became Prime Minister of Kenya; Charles Blondin was still walking tightropes; Dame May Whitty made her first film; the Marquis de Sade acquired a 15-year-old mistress.

At the age of 73
Dr Roget finished compiling his thesaurus (which he began at the age of 69); Konrad Adenauer became Chancellor of Germany; dog trainer Barbara Woodhouse began a world-wide dog training crusade

At the age of 74
S.J.Perelman, the humourist and scriptwriter for the Marx Brothers, drove from Paris to Peking in an old MG; Jean Cocteau decorated the church of Saint Blaise-des-Simples in Milly La Foret

At the age of 75
Ed Delano rode his bicycle 3,100 miles in 33 days to a reunion meeting; Nicholas Hawksmoor designed the towers of Westminster Abbey

At the age of 76
August Rodin married the girl with whom he had lived since he was 23; John XXIII became Pope

At the age of 77
Mahatma Gandhi took India to independence; Clara Burton served in Cuba in the Spanish-American war; John Glenn went into space and flew as a payload specialist on the Discovery mission

At the age of 78
H.G.Wells successfully submitted his doctoral thesis; Thomas
Beecham, the conductor, started a foreign tour; Mae West, the
American actress after whom the inflatable life vest was named,
appeared in the film Myra Breckinridge; Dame Edith Evans asked
that her age be removed from reference books because she feared
that it might prevent her getting work; Chevalier de Lamarck
proposed a new theory of evolution, suggesting that acquired
characteristics can be transmitted to the next generation

At the age of 79
Admiral Lord Cochrane volunteered for active service at the start of
the Crimean War; Dame Edith Evans was still appearing on stage in
New York; George Cayley invented a glider capable of carrying a
man (in 1853)

At the age of 80
Grandma Moses had her first solo art show; Levi Burlingham,
American jockey, rode in his last race; Marc Chagal created the sets
for the Metropolitan Opera's production of Mozart's 'Magic Flute';
Leopold Stokowski founded the American Symphony Orchestra (in
the same year he broke a leg playing football)

At the age of 81
Benjamin Franklin helped to write the American constitution;
Johann Goethe finished writing *Faust*; Marcus Cato decided to
destroy Carthage before it became a threat to the Roman Empire

At the age of 82
William Gladstone became British Prime Minister; Winston
Churchill published the first part of his four volume *A History of the
English Speaking Peoples*; American cowboy Bill Kane was still
riding in rodeos (though he won his last event at the age of 80);
Tolstoy was so fed up with all the people fussing around in his house
that he caught the first train out of town (sadly he became ill on the
train and died in a station master's cottage in the middle of nowhere)

At the age of 83

Charlie Chaplin received an Oscar; Dr Benjamin Spock was fighting for world peace

At the age of 84
American comedian and actor George Burns had his first hit record; Henri Matisse and Claude Monet were still painting; Somerset Maugham was still writing books

At the age of 85
Carl Jung finished work on *Man and his Symbols*, his best known work; Mae West made the film 'Sextette'; Theodore Mommsen received a Nobel Prize

At the age of 86
Louise Weiss was elected an MEP; Francis Rous received the Nobel Prize for identifying a virus which caused tumours in chickens; Elizabeth Blackwell, the first woman doctor, was still working; Jean Auguste Dominique Ingres was still painting

At the age of 87
Frank Lloyd Wright proposed building a skyscraper one mile high; Mary Baker Eddy founded the Christian Science Monitor; George Burns, comedian was still performing and telling jokes which he admitted were older than he was

At the age of 88
Michelangelo worked on the Rondanini Pieta; ex German Chancellor Konrad Adenauer started work on his memoirs; Pablos Casals, the cellist, was still giving concerts

At the age of 89
Philip W Whitcomb, a mature student, was awarded a degree from the University of Kansas; Dr Albert Schweitzer was still running his hospital in West Africa; Arthur Rubenstein, the pianist, was still giving concerts

At the age of 90
Leopold Stokowski, now recovered from his broken leg, recorded 20 albums, P.G.Wodehouse wrote the last Jeeves and Wooster book;

Pearl Taylor was chosen as Campus Queen at Long Beach City College where she was a student; Marc Chagall became the first living artist to be exhibited at the Louvre museum; Pablo Picasso was still drawing and engraving

And I could go on for much longer for many nonagenarians have achieved remarkable things. So, for example, at the age of 91 Alexander Baldine Kosloff was still teaching ballet, Thomas Hobbes was still writing books and Adolph Zukor was still chairman of Paramount Pictures. Antonio Stradivari was still making violins at the age of 93. George Bernard Shaw wrote his play *Why She Would Not* in seven days, just before his 94th birthday – he died at the age of 94 after falling from a tree he was pruning. Comedian George Burns was still performing at the age of 94. Bertrand Russell was still campaigning for peace at 94 – and he was in his 94th year when he set up the International War Crimes Tribunal in Stockholm. Japanese mountaineer and explorer Teichi Igarashi climbed Mt Fuji when he was 99. He did it again the following year, though he did carry a cane. He wore thick socks but no shoes.

Appendix 2

Granny Kennett's Pudding Club Recipes

With the permission of those named, I have included here a cluster of recipes for the most popular puddings served at the Duck and Puddle in Bilbury. These are traditional recipes which have been handed down through the generations. I take no responsibility for the accuracy of these recipes or the wisdom of making the puddings so described in the quantities listed here which, I confess, seem to me to be rather asking for trouble. Please note that all these puddings should be made from fresh ingredients (except for the two-day-old bread used in Mother Kennett's bread pudding) and cooked properly in some sort of oven.

1
Granny Kennett's Marmalade Pudding
(This recipe has been in the Kennett family for longer than anyone can remember.

Mix together a pound of breadcrumbs, a pound of sugar, eight eggs, a pound of finely chopped suet, chopped peel from three lemons and two jars of thick cut orange marmalade. Place the whole mixture in a pan and boil for several hours. When the mixture is nearly ready to serve, prepare a sauce with half a pound of butter, four ounces of sugar, two dozen almonds which have been chopped and ground and a third of a bottle of a good brandy. Beat the butter, sugar, almonds and brandy into a stiff creamy texture. When you serve the pudding, add the sauce around it. The pudding should be served with a good chunk of stilton cheese on a side plate and a glass of a decent port.

2
Mother Kennett's Bread and Butter Pudding

(Bread pudding recipes are two a penny and no old-fashioned recipe book is complete without one. There are probably more bread pudding recipes than there are recipes for cock-a-leekie soup. This recipe is recognised as having been the handiwork of Patsy's mother.)

Cut a loaf of two-day-old bread into thick slices and remove all the crusts. Make sure that there is no mould on the bread before cutting. It is important that the slices of bread should be cut quite thickly. Butter the bread on one side only, but very generously, making sure that the butter is rubbed well into the bread, and then spread lavish quantities of orange marmalade (preferably home-made but failing that any good brand will do) on top of the butter. Cut the bread into slices as though making soldiers for dipping into soft-boiled eggs and lay the slices in a buttered pudding dish. Beat three eggs into a pint of milk, pour the egg, and milk mixture on top of the slices of bread. The pudding should then be baked in the oven for half an hour or so. The pudding should be served with a very generous dollop of treacle gracing each portion. This pudding should serve two hungry people or four fussy eaters.

3
The Duck and Puddle Christmas Plum Pudding

(This recipe was specially created by Mrs Kennett (Patsy's Granny) for the Duck and Pudding some years ago and is now regularly served by Frank and Gilly at the pub. A decent plum pudding requires a good deal of work and preparation. Although this pudding was originally created to be served during the Christmas season, it is now so popular that it is served at the Duck and Puddle from the 20th September onwards. Just why the pudding is served from the 20th September is not known but it is commonly believed that it was probably the birthday of a villager who asked for the pudding to be served as a special treat.)

The Duck and Puddle Christmas Pudding requires two pounds of bread crumbs, two pounds of flour, two pounds of raisins, two pounds of currants, two pounds of suet, five ounces of freshly ground almonds, four ounces of grated lemon peel, four ounces of grated orange peel, a whole nutmeg which has been ground, half a pound of sugar, one and a half dozen large eggs, a pint of cream, a bottle of decent claret (it is always a mistake to use cheap wine when preparing a pudding) and a large wine glass full of a decent brandy. The ingredients should be mixed together in a large bowl and then placed in a pan and boiled for at least five hours. The pudding should be served with copious amounts of custard. A pudding of this size should provide sufficient portions for a medium sized family. If the pudding is being prepared for two or three people then the quantities can be halved. During the Christmas season, the Duck and Puddle serves this pudding every day for the Twelve Days of Christmas. In one recent year, Granny Kennett prepared 84 of these puddings for consumption by Duck and Puddle regulars over the Christmas holidays. (It should perhaps also be mentioned that during that same record period Peter Marshall sold 67 bottles of proprietary indigestion medicine. The doc did not keep a record of the amount of indigestion medicine he prescribed.)

4
Patsy Kennett's Apple Pudding
(This recipe was handed down to Patsy by her mother. Its origins are lost in the mists of Old Bilbury.)

A dozen and a half decent sized apples should be cut, sliced and macerated as though being prepared for an apple pie filling or for a sauce. A plain tin should be buttered and into it should be placed slices of bread which have been cut into small sections. The bread should line the whole of the pan, including the internal sides. Raisins, sultanas and chopped dates should be scattered over the bread. Melted butter should then be poured over the bread until it is well soaked. The macerated apple mush (as it is known locally) should be very well mixed with three quarters of a pound of sugar and the finely cut rind of two large lemons or three small ones and boiled for half an hour. The mush should then be poured into the bread-lined mould and put into the oven for three quarters of an hour or so. These quantities will serve four people with healthy appetites, six people with poor appetites, two very hungry farmhands or one Thumper Robinson. The apple pudding should be served with a sparkling white wine or, if the means are available, champagne.

5
Thumper's Favourite Tea-Time Snack.

(This pudding was originally prepared by Thumper's grandmother for her husband, Norris, a well-known North Devon farmer and accomplished trencherman. Norris went to London just once in his life (to deal with a legal problem concerning boundaries) but is still remembered at the Garrick club. Norris went there for lunch as a guest of his solicitor, who had travelled up to London with him, and proceeded to impress the other members by eating his way through the entire menu – including large portions of five different hot puddings.)

Chop up four apples, place them in a basin and add several large handfuls of breadcrumbs, a quarter of a pound of sugar, eight ounces of mixed currants and raisins and six beaten eggs. Add the finely chopped rind and the juice from two lemons and stir in two glasses of brandy or another alcoholic drink of choice. Tie a cloth over the top of the basin and boil it and the contents for several hours. The snack should be served with copious quantities of custard, thick slices of bread and butter and a pint of beer. This recipe serves one when prepared for Thumper Robinson but may serve more ordinary diners.

6. Granny Kennett's Spotted Dick

Political correctness means that in some recipe books and some eating establishments, this dish is now known as 'Spotted Richard'. However, the Kennett family in general, and Granny Kennett in particular, will have nothing to do with this nonsense. A spotted dick pudding is a spotted dick pudding is a spotted dick pudding and, for the Kennetts, and the rest of us in Bilbury, that will never change.

The basic ingredients for this version of spotted dick are one pound of plain flour, half a pound of well-shredded suet, a third of a pound of caster sugar, a tablespoonful of baking powder, three quarters of a pound of currants, the shaved peel of three lemons, four or five cloves and some milk. The suet, sugar, flour, baking powder, currants and lemon should be placed in a bowl and mixed very well. Milk should be added in sufficient quantity to turn the mixture into a soft and squidgy dough. The dough is then decanted into an ordinary pudding basin which has been greased with butter. A piece of muslin or greaseproof paper should then be placed over the top of the basin and tied in position with parcel string (not baler twine). A piece of cloth should then be tied on top of the muslin or greaseproof paper.

Again, the cloth should be tied with parcel string. The pudding basin should be placed in a large saucepan which is then two thirds filled with water, brought to the boil and simmered for quite a while. Granny Kennett always says that the simmering should last for at least an hour and a half, though some in the family claim that one hour should be enough. Water which is lost from the pan should be replaced as necessary. The cloths and string should then be removed and discarded. The pudding should be served on large plates (not in bowls) with huge quantities of freshly made custard poured on top so that it almost reaches the edge of the plate. To avoid spillage, the custard should be poured onto the spotted dick pudding when the plates have been placed on the table. These quantities should be sufficient to provide enough pudding for three or four people. If more guests are expected, then several puddings should be prepared. A spotted dick pudding should always be served with custard and never with cream or, heaven forbid, with ice cream.

Important Note from the author:
Please note that several of these puddings contain ingredients (such as alcohol) which might be unsuitable for some individuals. It should also be noted that those with weak digestive systems or modest appetites might find themselves over-faced by these dishes. These puddings are offered here in what are known in Devon as 'Bilbury quantities'. Some people, of a healthier and more sensible disposition, may prefer to reduce the quantities used in order to make smaller puddings.

Note from the author:
'If you have enjoyed this book I would be genuinely grateful (and forever encouraged) if you would be kind enough to leave a positive review on the Amazon product page.' – Vernon Coleman

There is more information about the author on his Amazon author page and at www.vernoncoleman.com

Made in the USA
Middletown, DE
20 May 2021